CITYSPOTS
BANG

C000319689

WHAT'S IN YOUR GUIDEBOOK?

Independent authors Impartial up-to-date information from our travel experts who meticulously source local knowledge.

Experience Thomas Cook's 165 years in the travel industry and guidebook publishing enriches every word with expertise you can trust.

Travel know-how Thomas Cook has thousands of staff working around the globe, all living and breathing travel.

Editors Travel-publishing professionals, pulling everything together to craft a perfect blend of words, pictures, maps and design.

You, the traveller We deliver a practical, no-nonsense approach to information, geared to how you really use it.

CITYSPOTS
BANGKOK

Written by Ryan Levitt
Updated by Gareth Marshall

Published by Thomas Cook Publishing
A division of Thomas Cook Tour Operations Limited
Company registration No: 1450464 England
The Thomas Cook Business Park, 9 Coningsby Road
Peterborough PE3 8SB, United Kingdom
Email: books@thomascook.com, Tel: +44 (0)1733 416477
www.thomascookpublishing.com

Produced by The Content Works Ltd
Aston Court, Kingsmead Business Park, Frederick Place
High Wycombe, Bucks HP11 1LA
www.thecontentworks.com

Series design based on an original concept by Studio 183 Limited

ISBN: 978-1-84848-173-2

First edition © 2007 Thomas Cook Publishing
This second edition © 2009 Thomas Cook Publishing
Text © Thomas Cook Publishing
Maps © Thomas Cook Publishing/PCGraphics (UK) Limited
Transport map © Communicarta Limited

Series Editor: Lucy Armstrong
Production/DTP: Steven Collins

Printed and bound in Spain by GraphyCems

Cover photography (Floating market in Damnoen Saduak)
© Vladimir Wrangel/BigStockPhoto.com

CONTENTS

SYMBOLS KEY

The following symbols are used throughout this book:

ⓐ address ⓣ telephone ⓦ website address ⓛ opening times
Ⓝ public transport connections ⓘ important

The following symbols are used on the maps:

ⓘ	information office	▦	points of interest
✈	airport	⭕	city
➕	hospital	⭕	large town
⬜	police station	○	small town
⬛	bus station	═	motorway
⬛	railway station	—	main road
Ⓜ	MRT Subway stop	—	minor road
Ⓜ	BTS Skytrain stop	—	railway
Ⓦ	Riverboat stop	❶	numbers denote featured
✝	cathedral		cafés & restaurants

Hotels and restaurants are graded by approximate price as follows:
£ budget price ££ mid-range price £££ expensive

▶ *The Grand Palace is still at the spiritual heart of Bangkok*

INTRODUCING
Bangkok

Introduction

Friendly, unpredictable, exhilarating, frustrating, hot, sweaty but most of all fun, Bangkok is a city that truly never stops. From early morning markets to late night clubs there is always someone on the move in this pulsating metropolis.

Initially you'll probably encounter sensory overload, with smells appealing to you one minute and appalling you the next. But Bangkok is all about experiences. Whether it's tearing through the streets in the back of a three-wheeled *tuk-tuk* or retreating to the spa and having the massage of a lifetime, you are sure to find something that makes you want to return.

A surprisingly friendly city considering the number of people living and working in its environs, help is always near at hand. Thais can be initially shy but soon warm to a smile, so remember: however hot, bothered or lost you feel, never lose your cool and you'll be treated like family.

Bangkok has become an increasingly popular destination for either short breaks or stopovers and there's plenty to keep you busy. It also represents great value for money as 5-star hotels are comparatively cheap, great food is all around, and there are plenty of market bargains to be had. It is, however, a city of contradictions with super rich and poor living together, no more better illustrated than when a chauffeur-driven Mercedes pulls up to a noodle stall offering meals for less than a pound.

Missing out on Bangkok would be missing out on one of life's great experiences, so whether it's culture, calm or kicks you desire, Bangkok has it all.

● *Bangkok is an intoxicating mix of the spiritual and the earthly*

When to go

Bangkok is a wonderful city to visit at almost any time of the year. Packed with festivals the capital offers great party opportunities throughout the year. For subdued and spiritual experiences, time your holiday to coincide with big events on the Buddhist calendar such as Visakha Bucha. A visit to the numerous temples will expose you to some memorable sights and envelop you in a cloud of incense.

Alternatively, royal functions always add a dash of pomp and colour. Watch out for lucky white elephants on these days as the King treats the people to street parties and entertainment.

SEASONS & CLIMATE

While it is enjoyable to visit Bangkok year-round, you may want to avoid the hot season from February to May, when the temperature can rise as high as 40°C (104°F). While it is possible to have fun in the city, the sweltering humidity will quickly sap you of your energy, confining most of your temple-hopping to the early morning or late afternoon when the sun isn't as baking.

The rainy season in the capital, as in the rest of the country, occurs from May to October. Downpours are severe, yet mercifully brief. Despite this, the regular drenchings can create havoc, making long-distance travel a bit of a nightmare. November to February are the months to visit if you want sunny, warm, clear days and breezy nights. Unfortunately, everyone and their mother travels during this time, and your empty poolside paradise could become a mob scene.

ANNUAL EVENTS

A strong respect for religion and love of a good time means that events and festivals are common activities in the land of smiles. For details on when and where to check things out, visit the Tourism Authority of Thailand website Ⓦ www.tourismthailand.org

⬥ *King Bhumibol Adulyadej, Rama IX of the Chakri dynasty, is revered by all Thais*

January–February
National Children's Day (Second Saturday in January) Go behind locked doors and visit sights normally closed to the public, including the inner Grand Palace. Child-focused locales such as amusement parks and zoos open their doors to children free of charge.

Chinese New Year Firecrackers pop, dragons roar and locals kick up their heels in celebration of a new year of luck and success. Head over to Chinatown to catch the bulk of the action.

February–March
Makha Bucha Follow Thais to the temples on this Buddhist high holiday that commemorates Buddha's last sermon before he reached nirvana.

May–June
Visakha Bucha Day A public holiday during which Thais celebrate Buddha's birth by visiting temples and making merry.

July–August
Asanha Bucha Young Thai men may look a little solemn on this day as their period as a monk begins. Temple visitation reaches a peak to honour Buddha's first sermon after enlightenment.

October
Vegetarian Festival Head to Chinatown for this festival of meat-free food that finds its roots in traditional Buddhist belief.

Ok Phansa The end of the rainy season is celebrated, along with the end of the Buddhist equivalent of Lent. Monks become more solemn as all hair on the eyebrows and scalps is shaved off.

November
Loy Krathong Tiny boats lit with candles and burning incense are set adrift on the Chao Phraya and the canals in this romantic full moon festival.

December
Bangkok Pride The gay community showers sequins in a celebration of sexuality.
King's birthday Head to Ratchadamnoen Road and Sanam Luang for the celebrations, although firework displays can be seen throughout the city.

PUBLIC HOLIDAYS
New Year's Day 1 Jan
Makha Bucha Day Feb–Mar
Chakri Day 6 Apr
Songkran (Thai New Year) 13–15 Apr
National Labour Day 1 May
Coronation Day 5 May
Royal Ploughing Day 9 May
Visakha Bucha Day May–June
Khao Phansa July
HM The Queen's Birthday 12 Aug
King Chulalongkorn Day 23 Oct
Ok Phansa Oct
HM The King's Birthday 5 Dec
Constitution Day 10 Dec

Songkran

If you thought New York's Times Square was nuts, then you've never been to Bangkok. The Thai New Year, celebrated every year from 13 to 15 April, is the party of the year – just be sure to dress appropriately if you want to take part in all the fun.

In its early incarnations, the festival was a celebration in honour of the hottest month of the year, when the sun entered Taurus. Practitioners would throw coloured powder or sprinkle Buddhas and monks with water as a sign of respect and honour. As time progressed, the water and powder throwing grew more intense, resulting in the free-for-all that you see today.

If you are in Bangkok as a tourist during Songkran, then be warned: you will get wet. As a Westerner, you are a prime target for Thais who think there is nothing better than covering you in buckets of water and coloured paint powder. Don't wear anything expensive; leave your best shoes and Chanel suit in your case for another day. Patpong and the Khao San Road are epicentres of the madness due to their large tourist populations.

As Songkran is a national public holiday, one of the nicest things about the period is the fact that half of Bangkok leaves the city. This is one of the only times during the year when driving is actually a pleasure and getting across town doesn't send you into a desperate frenzy.

No matter what happens during the festival, the key to survival is to do as the Thais do and smile. Arm yourself with a water pistol and aim at anything that moves (with a few obvious exceptions). If you do decide to retaliate, keep your wits about you, if you don't want to have a very wet weekend.

▲ *The wild excitement of Songkran*

History

While evidence of human settlement has been found around Bangkok as far back as the Cretaceous Age, the history of the Thai capital as an important metropolis can really only be traced to October 1767, following the defeat of the Thai people by the Burmese. The almost complete destruction of the former capital, Ayutthaya (see page 106), forced the Thai court to relocate, and King Taksin (1733–82) selected Thonburi as the site of his new palace.

Taksin, realising that he had to rebuild the Thai kingdom, quickly annexed much of Cambodia and the lost Ayutthaya territories. While he could have moved the capital back to Ayutthaya, he realised that Bangkok's convenient access to the Gulf of Thailand via the Chao Phraya River made the city a better option should threats rise again.

Despite Taksin's success on the battlefield, his 20 years of rule ended in rebellion. Angered by the introduction of bizarre laws and crippling taxes, the population rose up against him and he was executed following a coup. His death resulted in the creation of the Chakri dynasty and began Bangkok's golden age as Southeast Asia's most beautiful prize.

Rama I (1737–1809) moved the royal palace to the Eastern bank of the Chao Phraya early on during his reign due to its more defensible location and built numerous canals to assist with transport and movement of goods. Merchants pumped money into the new city and it quickly grew as villagers arrived in search of building work.

The Chakri dynasty were firm supporters of the arts and became great patrons of architects, writers, artists and dancers.

Most of the great temples of the city were built during this period under the watchful eye of the royal family.

As word of Thailand's beauty grew, European powers began to sniff around this potentially lucrative addition to their growing colonies. Fearing a complete loss of power, the Thais signed restrictive trade agreements with the English and allowed the French to grab their Cambodian territories. The eventual removal of territories in Malaysia, Laos and Cambodia may have caused great loss of face, but Thailand remained the only free nation in Southeast Asia.

King Chulalongkorn – the man made famous in *The King and I* – came to the throne in 1868 and introduced many Western influences into Thai culture, including the abolishment of slavery.

Political struggles during the 1930s and the Japanese invasion of 1942 plunged much of the nation into chaos as struggles for a democratic government ensued. In September 2006 a bloodless coup was carried out by the Royal Thai Army, who removed Prime Minister Thaksin Shinawatra while he was in New York at a UN meeting. A military appointed government was installed until fresh elections were carried out in late 2007. The winning party, held together by a coalition, had Thaksin's considerable wealth backing them, but the victory was tainted by corruption. A group calling themselves the People's Alliance for Democracy (PAD) blockaded Suvarnabhumi International Airport in a bid to bring the government down, and eventually the coalition partners switched to the opposition Democrat Party, led by Abhisit Vejjajiva, who formed a government in early 2009.

Lifestyle

It's a dog-eat-dog world out there – and no one knows this better than a resident of Bangkok. The Thai capital is a showcase of the finest objects money can buy and the results of extreme poverty wrapped up into one giant spring roll. Locals wake up every morning expecting a battle – through traffic, to find work, to make money and to have fun. Despite this, they manage to keep smiles on their faces at all times.

For years, government mismanagement has created a tradition of corruption that permeates every level of society. While you will never have to deal with it, due to your cushioned status as a tourist, be aware that it's there.

The Thai people are very strict Buddhists and the religion permeates every aspect of their daily routine. While riding a riverboat on the Chao Phraya River, you may see commuters busily *wai* (raise hands, palms together, to tip of chin) every time they pass a major temple. Elders are deeply respected and children are expected to look after their parents in their later years. Many locals don't actually come from Bangkok. Instead, they hail from surrounding villages and save up their baht to send back to their families back home.

All Thai men are expected to do at least a year of service as a monk – including royal princes. These saffron-robed young men can be seen throughout the city going about their daily tasks. If you are a woman, remember that any contact with a monk is forbidden. If you wish to pass something to a monk it must be done indirectly. Touching a monk is considered a terrible sin and will require the monk to go through an incredibly intricate cleansing ritual.

Political change is commonplace in Thailand and poses little, if any, danger to foreigners. At the height of disturbances in 2008 (see page 17) Bangkok functioned as normal and protests were restricted to a small part of the city until the airport was blockaded.

🔺 *Early morning yoga in Lumphini Park*

Culture

Unlike other cities in Asia, classical Western forms of artistic expression don't hold much sway over the hearts and minds of Bangkok's residents. Rather, locals support and respect the artistry of their own culture. Thai artistry is often expressed using dance/drama forms that base a lot of their movement in religious storytelling practices. Each eye movement or flick of the wrist conveys an emotion, thought or plot point. The overall look is spectacular, even if you don't quite understand everything that is being 'said' at all times.

Dance/drama can be divided into four subtypes, two of which you may find performed during your stay in Bangkok. *Likay* is the most popular form, due to its broadly comedic plots and lowest common denominator storylines. Despite this, *likay* is slowly declining in popularity as younger generations tune in to rival musical genres. *Lakhon* is the more serious of the two common dance/drama forms, with plot structures based strongly on Buddhist parables. The untrained eye may find the performances a little too melodramatic; however, the choreography will be sure to impress. Two other types of dance/drama – the regal masked *khon* and southern-influenced *manohra* – are seldom performed in the capital as their popularity wanes.

In a nation with a high rate of illiteracy, visual performance works best when trying to entertain large masses. There is a long Thai tradition of puppetry, specifically shadow puppetry and *nang yai* (a form of puppetry where the puppets, which have no moving parts, are manipulated by trained dancers). The art form continues in Bangkok at the **Joe Louis Theatre** in

○ Entrancing Thai dancers

the Suan Lum Night Bazaar (⒜ Rama IV Road, Lumphini
⒤ 02 252 2227 ⒧ From 13.00 for visiting; show: 20.00 Ⓝ MRT:
Lumphini. Admission charge). There are performances every
evening and the theatre can be visited in the afternoon.

Large theatre centres such as the National Theatre and
Bangkok Cultural Centre, while considered showpieces for
major visiting artists, lack a permanent calendar of events,
subscription season or effective marketing plans. As such,
they are poorly attended, despite their status as home to
such institutions as the Bangkok Symphony Orchestra.

Locals prefer their music of the folk variety and flock to
performances by grassroots singers over critically acclaimed
foreigners. One such form is *luuk thung*. This musical format
is highly rural and combines visual glitz with overwhelming
emotion. If Celine Dion sang country, then this would be the
Western equivalent.

If you're tempted to try to immerse yourself in Thai culture
by purchasing tickets to a touristy dinner-theatre performance,
then you are advised against it. Performers at these venues tend
to be very lacklustre, usually offering watered-down versions of
the real thing. Instead, ask around with locals to try to find out
when festivals or gigs are coming up. Many of the best events
are sold through word-of-mouth and not by using poster or
newspaper advertising campaigns. Still, it is useful to look out
for free listings magazine such as *BK magazine* and *Guru* for
up-to-date information on events around town.

⊙ *Traditional Thai dress*

Shopping

Choosing where to shop in Bangkok is almost (but not quite) as difficult as selecting what to buy. There are so many options you are likely to find markets setting up and stripping down at all times of the day and night. The Thai capital is known for its incredible array of goods for sale, including miraculous gems, lacquerware, stainless steel cutlery, gorgeous silks, and much, much more. Many visitors also flock here for fake designer goods; however, crackdowns by authorities are slowly limiting the number of faux watches and purses on display.

Shopping centres are a popular option, especially in hot weather. For computer and electrical goods head to **Panthip Plaza** (ⓐ New Phetburi Road ⓝ BTS: Ratchathewi) or for top designer brands try **Paragon** (ⓐ Siam Square ⓝ BTS: Siam). **MBK** (ⓐ Siam Square ⓝ BTS: National Stadium) has several floors offering

⬤ *You'll need a big suitcase for some of the souvenirs on sale*

CHATUCHAK WEEKEND MARKET (A.K.A. JJ MARKET)

Every weekend of the year transforms the scrappy market stalls of Chatuchak into a teeming mass of shoppers on the lookout for the bargain of a lifetime. Antiques, interiors, clothing, food, books – even pets – are all available for sale from over 8,000 sellers who stock the shelves with everything from designer goods to tat.

To survive a trip here, you'll need to come prepared. After all, over 250,000 people will be joining you in the packed, non-air-conditioned walkways. Bring lots of bottled water and get a really good night's sleep. Without it, the jostling and volume of humanity will fray your nerves in mere minutes.

Sections are colour- and symbol-coded, so if you are on the hunt for something specific, check the maps dotted throughout the complex. ⓐ Thanon Phahonyothin ⓘ 02 272 4440 ⓦ www.jatujakguide.com ⓒ 07.00–18.00 Sat & Sun ⓜ BTS: Mo Chit; MRT: Chatuchak Park

clothing, electrical and Thai crafts, while **Siam Square** itself (ⓝ BTS: Siam) is an outdoor warren of streets featuring local Thai designers catering mainly for the Thai market. For sheer fun, the night market at Patpong is a great option.

Finally, if you want something completely traditional, join a tour to one of the floating markets. Paddle while you purchase souvenirs and food items in a bustling atmosphere ringing with the sounds of haggling.

Eating & drinking

Hold on to your hats because the tastes and spices of Bangkok are sure to blow them right off your sweaty foreheads. Thai food is incredible – and offers more than just *pad thai* to tempt your palate. There are actually four main regional influences that dictate menu selection depending on where the chefs of your selected dining establishment hail from.

Northern Thai food is heavily based on exotically flavoured sauces and ingredients native to the region. Meat dishes are popular, including unique sausage combinations, curries and, especially, anything including pork.

Central Thai cuisine is much sweeter in taste, often combining the rich flavour of tropical fruits in sweet and sour combinations.

To the south you will find seafood and mouth-burning chillies. If you are new to Thai food, you may find some of the dishes too hot for your Western palate.

Most exotic are the flavours of the northeast. Isaan is an exceedingly poor region and families must make do, putting anything they can into the pot to survive. Don't be surprised to see insects, snakes and frogs on the menu in establishments that specialise in cuisine of this region. However, it is probably

PRICE CATEGORIES
Price ratings in this book are based on the average price of a two-course meal for one without drinks.
£ up to B100   **££** B100–300   **£££** over B300

⬆ *The smell of street vendors' cooking pervades Bangkok*

the most favoured food in Thailand with *som tam* (papaya salad), grilled chicken and sticky rice being a staple meal for many Thais.

One of the highlights of any visit to Thailand are the exotic specialities dished up on the street. You can find an incredible meal at virtually any hour of the day at the various stalls that line the streets of the Thai capital, dishing up everything from a Thai red curry with rice to grilled grasshoppers.

One of the best ways to select your eatery of the evening is to go where the locals go and follow the queues. Limiting yourself to safe, English-language establishments means that you'll be missing out on some of the best food in the city. Tourist-focused restaurants, while offering familiar surroundings and simple-to-understand menus, may be easier to enjoy – but the food is invariably of lesser quality.

If you do decide to partake in a streetside sensation, be sure to follow a few simple rules to ensure your meal doesn't result in your next bout of stomach upset. Watch the chef as he or she cooks the food. Ensure that the utensils they are using are clean and well maintained. Check that the food is thoroughly cooked before eating and avoid any fruits or vegetables that can't be peeled if you have any major concerns.

If you don't fancy the idea of yet another dish of Thai green curry, fear not. Bangkok is a great place to partake in the flavours of all of Asia. Certain streets and districts are well known for their Chinese, Japanese and Indian flavours. Chinatown is the place to head for if you have a craving for dumplings and dim sum. Japanese sushi and tempura can be found around the bars and eateries of Soi Thaniya – although many have strict entry policies that disallow Western tourists from entering. For Indian cuisine,

DO IT YOURSELF

If you love the flavours of Thailand, then why not bring them home with you? There are numerous cooking classes that offer the chance to learn from some of the nation's greatest chefs. For the best lessons, head straight for the school at The Oriental hotel (see page 40). Other good options to try are the **BaiPai Cooking School** (ⓐ Soi Naksuwan, Nonsi Road, Chong Nonsi ❶ 02 294 9029 ⓦ www.baipai.com ❶ 08.30–17.30 Tues–Sun) or the **Blue Elephant Cooking School** (ⓐ Blue Elephant Building, 233 Thanon Sathorn Tai ❶ 02 673 9353 ⓦ www.blueelephant.com ❶ 11.30–14.30, 18.30–22.30 ❷ BTS: Surasak).

head straight to the streets of Little India. Most establishments focus on the flavours of the north, particularly the Punjab, so variety may be slightly lacking when compared to – say – London's Brick Lane.

And if it's good, old-fashioned British food or American chain-style restaurants you yearn for, then you'll be in luck. You can pick up a burger and chips or slice of pizza on almost every street corner.

Entertainment & nightlife

When it comes to life after dark, Bangkok is a bit of a dichotomy. While the neon lights and drinking dens speak of a city that caters to the devilish and debauched, it also shuts firmly at 02.00. As soon as this early-morning hour hits, the shutters come down – and stay shut – until the sun begins to set on another day.

Despite these limitations, Thais love a good party. They also love a good drink. The tipple of choice is whisky and many establishments keep bottles for regular customers on hold on the shelves behind the bar.

After-hour clubs can be found all over the city in dark alleys and warehouse districts. Find them by making friends during your evening out. Eventually you'll be asked to join a back-alley party. Just hope the establishment is paying off the local police in order to avoid any inconvenient raids.

When drinking, it is customary to order food. Thais consider it socially untoward not to nibble while you glug. Don't be surprised if a new acquaintance forks out for a round of expensive cocktails and platters of food. To say no to their offerings is considered a sign of rudeness. If you become their guest for the evening, you will be expected to have fun – and

Patpong – Bangkok's famous district of sin

not to worry about payback. To offer a round in return would be considered an insult.

The exception to this rule is in nightclubs, which are often too packed to even consider holding anything other than a beer bottle. If you want to avoid any embarrassment while out with friends, be sure to bring some form of picture ID. Even if you have a touch of arthritis in your left knee and a head full of grey hair, you will be asked to produce some form of official identification.

Hip establishments have a lifespan of about six months until the next hot bar or district becomes the talk of the town. The rich of Bangkok are a very fickle lot and what is sizzling one day may be dead the next. Exceptions to this rule are anywhere in a 5-star hotel or with celebrity ownership connections, which are usually a good place to kick off the evening, such as the Bed Supperclub (see page 86) and the **Diplomat Bar** at the Conrad Hotel (ⓐ 87 Wireless Road, Phatumwan ⓣ 02 690 9999).

Live music options are less impressive in Bangkok than you might think. Musical selections are highly geared toward Asian bubble-gum pop – not fun unless you like pre-teen singers belting out numbers about puppy love. Jazz music remains popular, due to King Bumibol Rama IX's penchant for playing the saxophone – but performers of international calibre are few. Two of the better options are the **Saxophone** pub and restaurant (ⓐ Victory Monument ⓣ 02 246 5472 ⓦ www.saxophonepub.com ⓝ BTS: Victory Monument), which has nightly live jazz and blues music, and **Brown Sugar** (ⓐ Sarasin Road ⓣ 02 250 0103 ⓝ MRT: Lumphini), the oldest live jazz venue in Bangkok.

As in the rest of Asia, karaoke rules the roost in Bangkok when it comes to planning a night out with friends. Most

PATPONG

Some travel guides try to avoid any discussion about Patpong's legendary nightlife and concentrate on its official status as a night market, but everyone knows that is skirting the truth. While it's true that some visitors come to Patpong for knock-off designer goods of varying quality and cheap souvenirs, the majority arrive simply to stare at the human goods on offer.

This area of Bangkok has been synonymous with the sex trade since the days of the Vietnam War when American soldiers on leave would arrive here for 'R&R'. The girlie bars have been here ever since, although recent crackdowns have driven most of the really wild shows and venues away to streets like Soi Cowboy near Sukhumvit MRT station. ⓐ Patpong Soi 1 & 2, Thanon Silom ⓦ www.patpongnightlife.com ⓛ Night market: 19.00–late ⓜ BTS: Sala Daeng; MRT: Si Lom

establishments limit their English-language selection to a few tried and tested numbers. Unless you like *American Pie*, *Hotel California* or the complete works of Celine Dion, you may be out of luck.

Finally, there are the ever-popular hotel lounge acts. If you are tempted to stay for a listen, there is but one word of advice that can be given – don't. What you'll get for your efforts is exactly what you would expect if you were sitting in a suburban theme pub.

Sport & relaxation

SPECTATOR SPORTS

Football Football is a hit with young Thais; however, there are no teams worth making the effort to see unless a visiting British team decides to arrive in town. Thai fans are notoriously fickle when it comes to supporting their favourite team. Whereas you might see Arsenal all over the streets one season, it will be Liverpool the next. It all depends on who is on a winning streak at the time. You can follow the English Premier League in bars all over the city on weekend evenings as almost every game is shown live.

Muay Thai Spectator sports are extremely popular, particularly *Muay Thai*, a.k.a. Thai kickboxing. **Lumphini Stadium** (ⓐ Thanon Rama IV ⓣ 02 216 4373 ⓛ From 18.20 Tues & Fri, 17.00–20.00, 20.30–00.00 Sat ⓜ MRT: Lumphini) is a good place to catch bouts

🔺 Muay Thai *is passionately followed in Thailand*

involving everyone from complete amateurs to the best pros. Also try **Ratchadamnoen Stadium** (ⓐ Ratchadamnoen Nok Avenue ⓣ 02 281 4205 ⓛ 15.30–20.00 Mon, Wed & Thur, 15.30–20.00, 20.30–00.00 Sun). An ancient fighting format, Thai kickboxing is more than just about the battle. It combines religious honour, folk dance and respect for teachers in a ritual before the first kick is even thrown. To learn the art, contact the **Muay Thai Institute** (ⓐ Prachathipat, Thanyaburi, Pathum Thani (about 30–45 minutes out of Bangkok) ⓣ 02 992 0096).

PARTICIPATION SPORTS

When it comes to working out, Thais have two options: dawn or dusk. At any other time during daylight hours, the heat is too unbearable to consider a spot of exercise. Due to this environmental restriction, you'll often find groups of friends performing light routines in public parks when the temperatures are lowered. Lumphini Park (see page 90) is the most popular locale for city centre dwellers and there are plenty of trails, courts and open-air gyms where residents and visitors can hone their skills. If you have the inclination, why not give *takraw* a try. At first glance, it may look like a version of hacky sack, but this ball sport involves a net, hoop and lots of agility.

Golf Like their Japanese counterparts, Thais are huge fans of golf. If you fancy hitting a golf ball or two you are never far away from a driving range in Bangkok – look out for the huge nets. There are lots of golf shops near **Thaniya Plaza** (ⓝ BTS: Sala Daeng) where you can arrange a trip to a course, rent clubs or even organise lessons.

Accommodation

Bangkok offers incredible bargains and quality. If you've ever dreamed of splashing out on a luxurious hotel, then this is the place to do it. Time your visit right and you can find rooms in palace-like surroundings complete with rose petals scattered on the pillows and Egyptian cotton sheets for a lot less than you would imagine.

The Thai capital has long been a favourite destination for backpackers as these fantastic bargain-hunters know how to find a budget pad when they need one. The Khao San Road (Thanon Khao San) has long been the street of dreams for those with few funds. Once famous for its cockroach-infested dorms and sweat-stained sheets, the hotels on this strip are now some of the chicest in town.

Whereas in other cities, you get what you pay for, in Bangkok, you get much more. The only difference is how much pampering you can really stand.

HOTELS & HOSTELS

Atlanta Hotel £ For its combination of price and punch, the Atlanta can't be beaten. Once a favoured location among the elite back in the 50s, the hotel has experienced a resurgence thanks to its untouched retro interiors and authentically cool vintage feel. ➌ 78 Soi Sukhumvit 2 (Siam Square & Sukhumvit) ➊ 02 252 1650 ⓦ www.theatlantahotelbangkok.com ⓝ BTS: Nana

PRICE CATEGORIES
Hotels in Thailand are graded according to a star system running from 1 star for a cheap guesthouse to 5 stars for a luxurious property with numerous facilities. The ratings in this book are for a single night per double or twin room.
£ up to B2,500   **££** B2,500–5,000   **£££** over B5,000

Buddy Lodge £ This hotel kicked off the Khao San boutique trend that began around the time of the release of *The Beach*. In-room air-con, a small swimming pool and clean, simple furnishings make it a popular option for backpackers who want to splurge. 🅐 265 Thanon Khao San (Khao San, Phra Nakhon & Chinatown) 🅣 02 629 4477 🅦 www.buddylodge.com 🅝 Riverboat stop: Phra Arthit

Lub D £ Lub D, meaning 'sleep well', offers cool design, a mix of dorm rooms (including ladies-only area) and hotel rooms as well as free Wi-Fi and lots of security. It's like Khao San without the bustle. 🅐 4 Decho road, Suriyawong (Silom & Thonburi) 🅣 02 634 7999 🅦 www.lubd.com 🅝 BTS: Chong Nonsi

Reflections Rooms in Bangkok £ With art exhibitions a regular feature, Reflections is a little different. Bold and colourful rooms are individually designed by Thai artists. It is a 15-minute walk from Chatuchak weekend market. 🅐 224 Thanon Pradipat (Siam Square & Sukhumvit) 🅣 02 270 3344 🅦 www.reflections-thai.com 🅝 BTS: Saphan Khwai

Take a Nap £ Unique family-run hostel in which every room is individually designed with themes as varied as 'Let's Rock', 'Happy Forest' and 'Grand Palace'. Murals decorate the walls and Hua Lamphong train station is a short ride away. ⓐ Surawongse Junction, Rama IV Road (Silom & Thonburi) ⓣ 02 637 0015 ⓦ www.takeanaphotel.com ⓝ BTS: Sala Daeng; MRT: Sam Yan

Viengtai Hotel £ Popular with budget tour operators, this multi-storey hotel was one of the first in the area. Interiors feel a tad dated due to the almost constant use, but amenities such as air conditioning and a small swimming pool make it a good option. Rooms are clean, if a little minimal. ⓐ 42 Rambuttri Road (Khao San, Phra Nakhon & Chinatown) ⓣ 02 280 5434 ⓦ www.viengtai.co.th ⓝ Riverboat stop: Phra Arthit

The Heritage Baan Silom £–££ Neo-colonial style buildings merged with modern technology define this boutique hotel. Bright, well-appointed rooms give it a touch of class. ⓐ 659 Silom 19, Silom Road (Silom & Thonburi) ⓣ 02 236 8388 ⓦ www.theheritagebaansilom.com ⓝ BTS: Chong Nonsi

The Davis ££ Boutique hotel options got a kick up the backside when this hotel opened. Choose from traditional Thai-style accommodation or luxury rooms in the main building. ⓐ 88 Soi Sukhumvit 24 (Siam Square & Sukhumvit) ⓣ 02 260 8000 ⓦ www.davisbangkok.net ⓝ BTS: Phrom Phong

Dream Hotel ££ An ultra-cool hotel that claims to be a dream and it can be quite surreal at times but it never falters on service. Stuffed tigers patrol the lobby while preloaded iPods can be requested at check-in. ⓐ 10 Soi Sukhumvit 15 (Siam Square & Sukhumvit) ⓣ 02 254 8500 ⓦ www.dreambkk.com ⓝ BTS: Asok; MRT: Sukhumvit

Dusit Thani ££ The first modern 5-star hotel in Bangkok is still a treasure after a recent modernisation. Looking onto Lumphini Park, and next to both BTS and MRT stations, it is well-placed for exploring the city. ⓐ 946 Thanon Rama IV (Silom & Thonburi) ⓣ 02 200 9000 ⓦ www.dusit.com ⓝ BTS: Sala Daeng; MRT: Si Lom

⬤ The Oriental is one of the world's most luxurious hotels

Luxx ££ This small converted shop-house is hip and trendy with zen-like rooms to match. Luxuriously set with large, comfy beds, cooling wooden floors and DVD players it almost feels like home. ⓐ 6/11 Decho Road, Suriyawong (Silom & Thonburi) ⓣ 02 635 8800 ⓦ www.staywithluxx.com ⓝ BTS: Chong Nonsi

The Oriental £££ Consistently ranked among the best hotels in the world, The Oriental has long been the benchmark for Bangkok's plethora of luxury hotels. ⓐ 48 Oriental Avenue, off Thanon Charoen Krung (Silom & Thonburi) ⓣ 02 659 9000 ⓦ www.mandarinoriental.com ⓝ Riverboat stop: Oriental

The Peninsula £££ Breathtaking views of the river and city skyline along with outstanding service ensure The Peninsula remains a favourite of the rich and famous. ⓐ 333 Thanon Charoen Nakorn (Silom & Thonburi) ⓣ 02 861 2888 ⓦ www.peninsula.com ⓝ BTS: Saphan Taksin, then catch shuttle boat

The Sukhothai £££ A modern hotel that never forgets its Thai influence. So spacious you could almost feel like you are the only person there. ⓐ 13/3 Thanon South Sathorn (Silom & Thonburi) ⓣ 02 344 8888 ⓦ www.sukhothai.com ⓝ MRT: Lumphini

GUESTHOUSES

Baan Soi Sukhumvit 18 £ Small, boutique-style guesthouse with a family feel. Peaceful setting but just a short walk from public transport. The rooftop garden is great for watching the city go by. ⓐ 3/13-14 Soi Sukhumvit, 18 Sukhumvit Rd (Siam Square

& Sukhumvit) ☎ 02 204 0301 🌐 www.baansukhumvit.com
Ⓝ BTS: Asok; MRT: Sukhumvit

Bangkok Christian Guesthouse £ This simple guesthouse provides
large, clean rooms to weary travellers. ⓐ 123 Soi Sala Daeng 2
(Silom & Thonburi) ☎ 02 233 6303 🌐 www.bcgh.org Ⓝ BTS: Sala
Daeng; MRT: Si Lom

Suk11 Guesthouse £ Well-designed traditional teak guesthouse
offering both dorm-style and private rooms. Beware of thin walls
that tend to carry noise. ⓐ 1/33 Soi Sukhumvit 11 (Siam Square
& Sukhumvit) ☎ 02 253 5927 🌐 www.suk11.com Ⓝ BTS: Nana

Tuptim Bed & Breakfast £ Cheap and cheerful place just off
Khao San Road. Bathrooms are shared but all rooms have air
conditioning. ⓐ 82 Rambuttri Road (Khao San, Phra Nakhon
& Chinatown) ☎ 02 629 1535 🌐 www.tuptimb-b.com
Ⓝ Riverboat stop: Phra Arthit

Baan Chantra £–££ A few blocks from Khao San Road, this
traditional Thai home takes a step back in time giving an idea of
how Bangkok once looked. ⓐ 120/1 Samsen Road (Khao San, Phra
Nakhon & Chinatown) ☎ 02 628 6988 🌐 www.baanchantra.com
Ⓝ Riverboat stop: Phra Arthit

THE BEST OF BANGKOK

Bangkok provides the best of everything – great food, fantastic shopping, cultural opportunities galore and gripping sporting matches. Whether you're a fan of late nights and partying till dawn or daytime neighbourhood explorations, you're sure to find plenty of things to fill your holiday no matter how long you decide to stay.

TOP 10 ATTRACTIONS

- **Chao Phraya River** The Chao Phraya River is Bangkok's lifeblood and the buzz of activity never stops. Hop on a riverboat ferry to see the city come to life (see page 94)

- **Grand Palace** This massive complex made up of temples and museums is the most important structure in the city (see page 64)

- **Jim Thompson's House** This ex-CIA operative single-handedly rebuilt the Thai silk industry. His former home is a masterpiece of traditional teak house construction (see page 82)

- **Wat Arun** At sunset, this glorious temple with its massive column looms over the river below, providing spectacular views of the water traffic (see page 97)

- **Chatuchak Weekend Market** Fantastic fashions, fabulous food and scintillating souvenirs – it's all here in the chaos. See what treasures you can find (see page 25)

- *Muay Thai* Combining dance, agility, grace, power and honour, *Muay Thai* kickboxing is a fascinating sport both to watch and to practise (see page 34)

- **The Oriental** You can almost feel the colonial era dripping out of the walls of this luxury hotel. From Noel Coward to Somerset Maugham, all the big names of their era have stayed here (see page 40)

- **Patpong** Whether or not the ladies and gentlemen of Patpong attract you, the neon glitz of this district of sin has to be seen to be believed (see page 33)

- **Khao San Road** Backpackers have been calling this road home for over two decades. No longer a collection of flophouses and cheap eats, it is now one of the hottest night-time neighbourhoods in town (see page 76)

- **Wat Pho** The temple itself may not inspire, but the incredible masseurs taught at the on-site academy will knead your muscles to nirvana (see page 66)

⬇ *Thai fruit stalls are a riot of colour*

Suggested itineraries

HALF-DAY: BANGKOK IN A HURRY

Grab a riverboat and ply the waves up the Chao Phraya River to see the communities that line its life-giving banks. The views from the river, of the hotels near King Taksin Bridge and the Grand Palace hugging the shores of Phra Nakhon, are sure to seduce and captivate you.

1-DAY: TIME TO SEE A LITTLE MORE

Get off the boat at Tha Chang and explore the grounds of the Grand Palace. If time permits, head up the street to see the artefacts of the National Museum – a treasure trove of Southeast Asian art and culture.

2–3 DAYS: TIME TO SEE MUCH MORE

Try to time your visit to include a weekend so you can shop till you drop at Chatuchak. Be sure to enjoy a massage during your temple hops or get the adrenalin pumping by heading over to Lumphini Stadium to see a bout or two of *Muay Thai*.

LONGER: ENJOYING BANGKOK TO THE FULL

Get more out of your holiday by getting out of town. See the UNESCO World Heritage Site of Bangkok's glorious former capital city at Ayutthaya and combine it with a trip to one of the famous floating markets. Alternatively, top up your tan on the beaches of Pattaya, Bangkok's favoured all-season playground.

● *Find time to visit the peace and the gilt of the Grand Palace*

Something for nothing

First, the bad news. If you're looking to get something for free in Bangkok, then you'll be in trouble. Bangkok is a city of survival. If you want to see the sights or get around, you'll need baht in your pocket and a lot of haggling power. Now for the good news. You may have to pay for everything, but almost every experience is well within the budget of even the very broke. One of the best ways of getting to grips with the city is by taking a riverboat ferry up the Chao Phraya River. For a journey between the Taksin Bridge and Tha Chang, expect to pay between 10 and 30 baht. The Chao Phraya Express Boat (see page 94) is a special hop-on, hop-off service allowing unlimited trips along the river for 150 baht.

If that doesn't float your boat, you can always grab a *tuk-tuk* to see Bangkok's alleys and avenues. About 100 baht will be more than enough to cover numerous blocks within the city.

For outdoor pursuits and a chance to mix and mingle with locals, Lumphini Park is the place to go. Arrive in the early hours and you'll be able to join a group practicing *t'ai chi*.

Temple-hopping is a must-do item on every visitor's list; entry fees range from completely free to 200 baht. Offerings are, of course, extra. Exceptions are the Grand Palace and Wat Phra Kaew, where entry tickets are more expensive.

By night, wandering among the streets of Patpong provides a great visual spectacle – right on the street. While a beer at one of the bars or a streetside snack will add to the fun, you don't need to sup and sin to admire the atmosphere.

Finally, if all else fails, find a reputable massage parlour and lie down for the rubdown of your life. Some of the best practitioners provide amazing treatments for just £4 an hour.

🔺 *A river trip is a great way to see Bangkok for next to nothing*

When it rains

When it rains in Bangkok – and it almost certainly will if you visit between May and October – then don't worry. While the potholed streets turn to mush and parks get flooded, there are still plenty of things to see and do that won't involve ruining your Manolo Blahniks.

One of the most enjoyable things to do is a spot of shopping in the connected malls that line Thanon Rama I between National Stadium and Chit Lom BTS stations. While the department stores and shopping centres themselves aren't particularly inspiring, there are a number of local outlets which offer unique clothes, furnishings and food goodies. The fact that the malls are air conditioned in this city of almost permanent humidity adds to the enjoyment factor.

If shopping doesn't do it for you, then you can always kill an hour or two with a massage. For high-end pampering, head straight for the spas at the Dusit Thani, Banyan Tree or Oriental hotels. Facilities at each of these properties are sublime; however, you'll have to pay through the nose for the heavenly privilege. Alternatively, head to Wat Pho and its school of traditional medicine and massage. While the rooms used won't be as pleasing to the eye, the touch will be pleasing to the body as the therapists are all trained to high standards.

For something a little more active, why not get tickets to see a bout of Thai boxing? *Muay Thai* (see page 34) is an ancient sport that combines agility, strength and honour in one complete package. All bouts feature a ritual dance to kick off the match in order to show respect to the fighters' schools and teachers.

A live band accompanies the action, picking up the pace using ever-increasing rhythms as the match goes on. Lumphini Stadium is the place to go to catch the best practitioners.

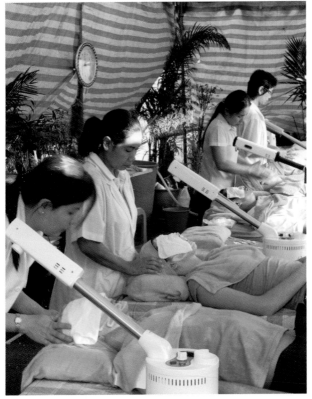

🔺 *The bliss of a Thai massage*

On arrival

TIME DIFFERENCE

Bangkok time is seven hours ahead of Greenwich Mean Time. Daylight saving does not apply, so during British Summer Time clocks in Bangkok will only be six hours ahead of those in the UK.

ARRIVING

By air

Travellers arriving in Bangkok from abroad will land at Suvarnabhumi Airport, located 25 km (15 ½ miles) east of the city in Nong Ngu Hao (Cobra Swamp). The airport opened in late 2006 and now handles all international flights. Note that some domestic services still run from the old airport at Don Muang. Check the departure airport carefully if you have booked a connecting flight or a flight out of Bangkok to another city in China, as it's easier than you might imagine to go to the wrong airport and miss your flight.

Depending on traffic – and it will always be at some level of horrible – a taxi to the city centre will cost B150–250 plus an airport surcharge of B50. An express bus service is also available for those on a really tight budget, with tickets costing B150. Four separate routes take you to Silom, Khao San Road, Sukhumvit or Hua Lamphong train station. A new fast rail link between the city and airport is in the process of opening. When fully functional, it will service the Phaya Thai BTS station and the Petchaburi MRT station at the City Air Terminal in Makkasan.

Suvarnabhumi Airport ☏ 02 123 1888
ⓦ www.bangkokairportonline.com
Don Muang Airport ⓦ www.donmuangairportonline.com

By rail

If you are embarking on a trip across Southeast Asia, you may arrive at Bangkok's Hua Lamphong Station as part of your journey. Trains are operated by the State Railway of Thailand and come in from as far south as Singapore and north from Chiang Mai. Destinations in Cambodia, Laos, Burma, China and Vietnam are

⬤ Tuk-tuks *are a fun way to get around in Bangkok – haggling is essential*

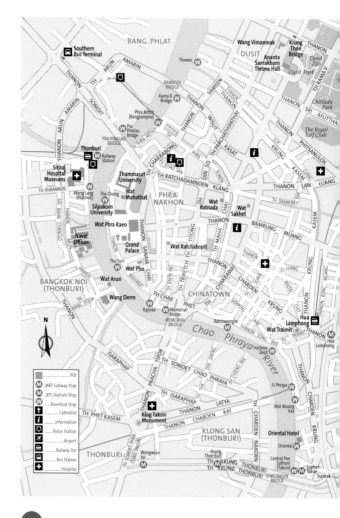

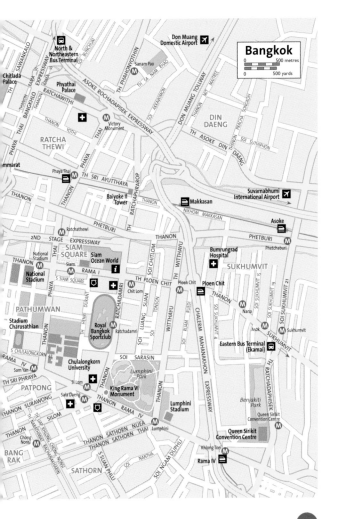

not served due to border restrictions. The train service in Thailand isn't rapid; however, it does help you avoid the crippling traffic for which the city is famous.

By road

Getting to your destination by road is sure to test your patience as traffic will probably double your projected journey time. Depending on where you are coming from, long-distance coach services will drop you off at the Eastern, Southern or Northern & Northeastern bus terminals (see page 131), from where it is easy to pick up a taxi or *tuk-tuk* into town.

FINDING YOUR FEET

Getting around Bangkok is a challenge. The streets are hot, humid and packed with cars, street signs are confusing, pedestrian crossings are almost non-existent and drivers ignore basic laws. If you're lost, wend your way to the Chao Phraya River, which acts as the heart of the city. *Tuk-tuks* – a colourful form of open-air taxi – can help you get to your destination quicker by whizzing their way through tighter spaces.

ORIENTATION

Bangkok never had the luxury of planning and as a result is a warren of small streets, or *sois* as they are commonly known. This lack of planning is still evident today and you'll see old buildings being pulled down and new ones erected swiftly in their place.

Fortunately there are a few points of reference that help you find your bearings. The river is a good place to start as the bulk of the city lies between Saphan Taksin (King Taksin Bridge) and Krung Thon Bridge, just a little north of Khao San Road. Travelling along the river, Bangkok sits on the east of the river and going from north to south you'll pass treasures such as the Grand Palace and Wat Arun before hitting the more commercial area of Chinatown and finally the splendour of the big name 5-star hotels of The Oriental and Peninsula.

For landmarks in the city, you should always be in sight of Baiyoke II Tower, the city's tallest building, giving a good point of reference wherever you are.

GETTING AROUND

The best way to navigate the centre of the city is by hopping on the Skytrain, usually known as the **BTS** (ⓦ www.bts.co.th). Adding to the concrete jungle that is Bangkok, this train slices its way through city streets perched on huge legs of concrete. Don't let that put you off. Fast, reliable and spotlessly clean, the two BTS routes 'Silom' and 'Sukhumvit' cover these two business and residential areas, joining in the city centre at Siam Square.

The underground subway system is known as the **MRT** (ⓦ www.mrta.co.th) and is also useful for getting around the city centre. At various points along the BTS routes there are MRT interchanges, but the BTS affords such great views of the city it's worth using as much as possible.

Journey prices range from 15 to 40 baht on the BTS and 14 to 42 baht on the MRT. The BTS has a range of ticketing options, including the useful day pass for 120 baht. The MRT has only single trip tickets and a card which you can load with money and use until it runs out. Unfortunately there is no joint ticketing system

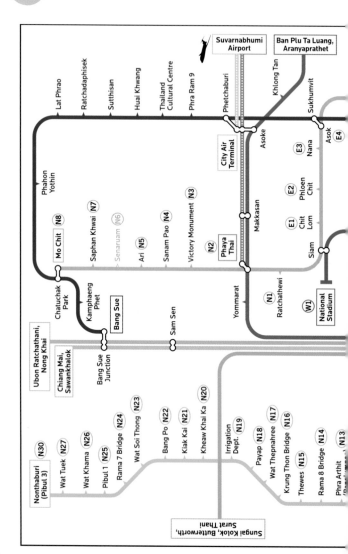

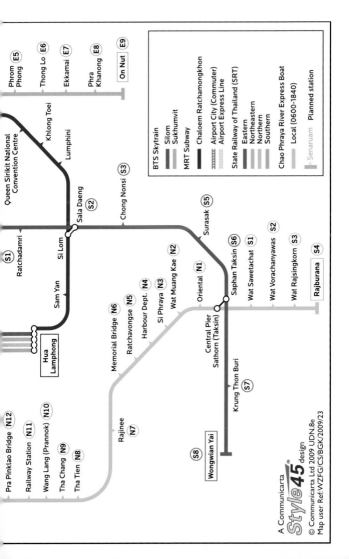

as yet. For help buying tickets, visit one of the BTS information centres at Siam, Nana and Saphan Taksin stations.

A more exciting option is to take the Chao Phraya River Express Boats up the river (see page 94). Little boats also operate river crossings continually throughout the day. Khlongs, or canal boats, are smaller with a more informal service, but can be useful for reaching certain destinations. All stops mentioned in this guide are official Chao Phraya River Express Boats stops.

When possible, use the BTS Skytrain, MRT Subway system or riverboats to get around the city. Bangkok's choking traffic will keep you crawling for hours if you try to get anywhere during the rush hour. Remember, if you are a woman and you see a monk, keep well away from him as he cannot be touched by you. Many public transport systems reserve private areas for the use of monks only.

If you are travelling further afield, Bangkok's various train lines may be useful. For rail timetables and fares from Hua Lamphong station, call ☎ 02 222 0175 or check the English-language section of ⓦ www.railway.co.th.

CAR HIRE
As traffic is so horrendous and street signs have limited English-language translations, it is not advised to rent a car. Should you wish to get out of town, private taxis are extremely affordable and will save you time and any attacks on your patience levels.

● *Wat Pho is a favourite with tourists*

Khao San, Phra Nakhon & Chinatown

From the backpacker-oriented guesthouses in the north to bustling Chinatown in the south, this part of Bangkok is the heart of the city – with the Grand Palace acting as the pulsing organ from which everything revolves. The King of Siam founded the city on the banks of the Chao Phraya and the results can be seen today in the wealth of temples and palaces that currently call the district home.

Chinatown is merchant central. Packed with shops and restaurants, it's a buzzy neighbourhood that will spark your senses down every alley.

Khao San has long been known as a traveller's mecca and it continues to be a central point for anyone passing through Asia. Whether you want to pick up some essentials, check out your next trip or chill out with fellow adventurers, you can find it all here.

SIGHTS & ATTRACTIONS

Ananta Samakhom Throne Hall

Now only used for state occasions, this impressive reception hall is a sea of gilt made to impress all visiting dignitaries who enter. You'll be just as awed. ⓐ Thanon U-Thong Nai ❶ 02 628 6300 ⓦ www.vimanmek.com ❶ 10.00–20.00 ⓝ Riverboat stop: Thewes; bus: 503. Admission charge

Devasathan

The original location of a giant swing whose remains can now be seen at Wat Suthat, this collection of three shrines was built in 1784 and is important as a chronicle of the period when Brahminism combined with Buddhism in religious practice. ⓐ 268 Thanon Din So ⏰ 08.00–18.00 🅽 Riverboat stop: Tha Chang

Dusit Park

This park is Bangkok's green lung, packed with museums and landmark buildings that chronicle the history and artistry of Thailand as a nation. The highlight of any visit is a tour of Wang Vimanmak, the former palace of Rama V. There are also museums that display exhibits of royal ceremony archives, ancient cloth and lucky white elephant remains. ⓐ 16 Thanon Ratchawithi ⓘ 02 628 6300 ⏰ 09.30–16.00 🅽 Bus: 515, 542

Dusit Zoo

Don't go to this zoo if you're uncomfortable with small pens and bland enclosures. Instead, it's the various amusement rides and gardens that should attract you – especially if you have kids. ⓐ 71 Thanon Rama V ⓘ 02 281 2000 🆆 www.dusitzoo.org ⏰ 08.00–18.00 🅽 Bus: 515, 542. Admission charge

Lak Muang (City Pillar Shrine)

Thais are very superstitious people, and much of what is planned on the calendar goes according to what the astrological chart says will be an auspicious day. Lak Muang is where the city horoscope is kept – in fact, it was built even before construction of the Grand Palace began. As people believe the shrine is a place where wishes are granted, it is packed throughout the day.

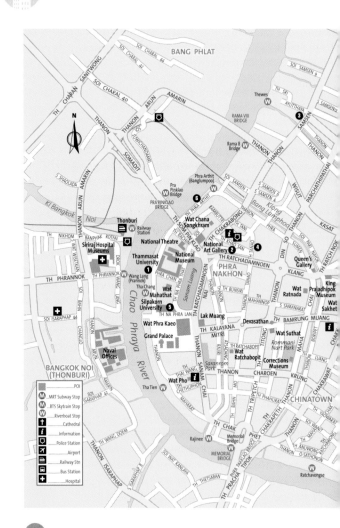

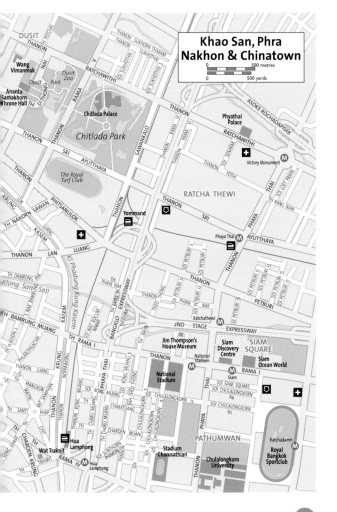

Thanon Sanam Chai 02 222 9876 05.30–19.30 Riverboat stop: Tha Chang

THE EMERALD BUDDHA

Two of Bangkok's greatest attractions are the Grand Palace and the Wat Phra Kaeo (Temple of the Emerald Buddha). Once a home for Thai kings, the Grand Palace was built in 1782 by Rama I when he moved the Thai capital here from Thonburi across the river. The building was designed to resemble an older palace in an earlier capital, Ayutthaya, and it became both his residence and the centre of government. Rama I also ordered the erection of the Temple of the Emerald Buddha, which was used both as the royal temple and as his personal place of worship. The Grand Palace is still very much in use, although mainly for ceremonial duties as the current king resides at Chitralada Palace.

The Emerald Buddha is the most revered image of the Buddha in Thailand, which explains why this temple is the most sacred in the country. The Emerald Buddha has had quite a history and has passed between leaders throughout the region over the years. Both Cambodia and Laos believe their temples are the true resting place for the Buddha.

Shorts, sandals and bare shoulders are strictly forbidden; however, suitably modest clothing is available for hire at the entrance should you forget. Thanon Na Phra Lan 02 222 8181 08.30–15.30 Riverboat stop: Tha Chang. Admission charge

Sanam Luang (Phramen Ground)

This plot of parkland has had numerous uses during its history. First the site for royal cremations, then a golf and race course, then the site of the weekend market that now lies at Chatuchak in the north of the city, it is now best known as the location for the Royal Ploughing Ceremony each May. Farmers across the nation await this day with breathless anticipation, as they are not permitted to start preparing their land for rice cultivation until the ceremony is complete. ⓐ North of Grand Palace across Nha Phra Lan Road ⓒ 24 hrs ⓝ Riverboat stop: Tha Chang

Saranrom Park

Popular public park that used to be the private garden of a royal palace. At sunrise and sunset, the space positively heaves with exercise addicts. ⓐ Thanon Charoen Krung ⓒ 05.00–21.00 ⓝ Riverboat stop: Tha Tien

Silpakorn University

Considered the finest college of fine arts in Thailand, this institution holds a gallery of works created by former masters and artists-in-residence, in addition to regular exhibitions of pieces created by current students. ⓐ 31 Thanon Na Phra Lan ⓣ 02 623 6115 ⓦ www.su.ac.th ⓒ 08.30–16.30 Mon–Fri ⓝ Riverboat stop: Tha Chang

Thammasat University

If you are interested in Thai politics, then you may recall the notorious student demonstrations of 1973. Thammasat university has always been known as a location of active student dissent and should therefore be avoided if any political instability is affecting the city. 2 Thanon Phra Chan 02 221 6111 www.tu.ac.th 08.30–16.30 Riverboat stop: Tha Chang

Wat Pho (Temple of the Reclining Buddha)

Wat Pho is the largest *wat* in Bangkok and is famous in tourist circles due to its massive gold-plated Buddha statue measuring over 46 m (50 yards) in length. Take a close look at the soles of the Buddha's feet to see intricate mother-of-pearl inlay work. Locals come to Wat Pho due to its history as a centre for the teaching of traditional Thai massage. Many claim that the massage therapists around this temple offer the best massages in all of Thailand. Thanon Sanam Chai 02 221 2974 www.watpho.com 08.00–17.00 Riverboat stop: Tha Tien. Admission charge

Wat Sakhet (Temple of the Golden Mount)

Wat Sakhet is famous primarily as the site of the Golden Mount, from which incredible views of the city can be enjoyed. Two spiral paths lead up and down from the top of this hill, which was artificially created from dirt and rubble unearthed during canal diggings. 344 Chakkaphatdi Phong 02 223 4561 www.watsrakesa.com 08.00–17.00 Riverboat stop: Tha Chang. Admission charge for Golden Mount only

CULTURE

Corrections Museum

Located in a public park on the site of a former jail, the Corrections Museum is a gruesome stop for even the most hard-hearted.

◯ *Don't miss the astonishing gold-plated Buddha in Wat Pho*

Displays include various instruments of torture and punishment.
🅐 Thanon Maha Chai 🕿 02 226 1704 🅦 www.correct.go.th/eng.htm
🕒 09.00–16.00 Mon–Fri 🅝 Riverboat stop: Memorial Bridge

King Prajadhipok Museum

The transition of government from absolute monarchy to
democracy during the reign of Rama VII was one of the most
turbulent periods in Thai history. This museum takes a look at
the social and political changes that occurred during the period,
using multimedia displays in a non-biased manner. 🅐 2 Thanon
Lan Luang 🕿 02 280 3413 🕒 09.00–16.00 Tues–Sun 🅝 Riverboat
stop: Tha Chang. Admission charge

National Art Gallery

This museum is interesting to those who have a desire to see
what contemporary Thai art looks like, but can be missed if you
only have a limited amount of time. Housed in the former Royal
Mint, it sometimes hosts big-name temporary collections. Check
listings to see what's on while you're in town. To reach Thanon
Chao Fa, walk along Pha Athit road and turn left just before
the bridge. Continue on this road; the museum is on the left.
🅐 5 Thanon Chao Fa 🕿 02 224 1396 🕒 09.00–16.00 Wed–Sun
🅦 www.rama9art.org 🅝 Riverboat stop: Phra Arthit.
Admission charge

National Museum

This 'must-do' museum is the largest in Southeast Asia and
boasts a collection of Thai art that is beyond compare. Numerous
relics chart Thai history through the years of rule when the former

capitals of Ayutthaya and Sukhothai ruled over the empire. Information is sadly lacking on most of the displays, so if you want to know more detail about the art and artefacts, either join a tour or pick up a copy of the guide available when you purchase your ticket. ⓐ 4 Thanon Na Phra That ⓣ 02 224 1333 ⓦ www.thailandmuseum.com ⓛ 09.00–16.00 Wed–Sun ⓝ Riverboat stop: Tha Chang. Admission charge

Queen's Gallery

Dedicated to Thailand's beloved Queen Sirikit, this museum houses temporary exhibits from both big-name Thai and international artists. ⓐ 101 Thanon Ratchadamnoen Klang ⓣ 02 281 5360 ⓦ www.queengallery.org ⓛ 10.00–19.00 Mon, Tues, Thur–Sun ⓝ Riverboat stop: Tha Chang

RETAIL THERAPY

Amulet Market Pick up a lucky charm at this market located adjacent to Wat Mahathat. Prepare to haggle heavily for a good price. ⓐ Trok Wat Mahathat, Thanon Maharat ⓛ 09.00–18.00 ⓝ Riverboat stop: Tha Chang

Bo Bae Market Great market find for those in need of funky clothes for less cash. Quality varies from cheap chic to near designer. Prepare to hunt hard. ⓐ Soi Rong Muang, Thanon Krung Kasem ⓛ 09.00–18.00 ⓝ Riverboat stop: Phra Arthit

Pak Klong Market If you love the floral bracelets and necklaces you are offered when you check into a Thai hotel or simply adore the fragrance of exotic blooms then head to this round-the-clock flower market that combines great prices with an authentically Thai feel. Thanon Chak Phet between Memorial Bridge and Klong Lord 🕐 24 hrs Ⓝ Riverboat stop: Rajinee

Phahurat Market Indian treasures galore in this market brimming with objects from the subcontinent. Food, silks and trinkets are all available for less than the cost of a Bollywood film ticket. Thanon Chakrapeth 🕐 09.00–18.00 Ⓝ Riverboat stop: Memorial Bridge

Sampeng Market This market is the unofficial heart of Chinatown. A trip here will feel like you've just arrived in the back streets of Beijing or Hong Kong. Everything from clothes to housewares can be picked up at very good rates – you'll have to bargain hard for the best prices. Soi Wanit 1 🕐 09.00–18.00 Ⓝ Riverboat stop: Ratchavongse

Saphan Phut This night market is a hit with fans of kitsch costume jewellery and slogan t-shirts. A great place for plastic fantastic fun and frivolity. Thanon Tripetch 🕐 20.00–00.00 Ⓝ Riverboat stop: Memorial Bridge

Thanon Yaowarat The main street of Chinatown is a buzzing mass of energy. Pop into the gem stores, get a herbal remedy, admire some hand-wrought cutlery or pick up a cheap mobile. Almost every shop or service you could ever need is available here. Just watch for traffic and pickpockets. Ⓝ MRT: Hua Lamphong

⬤ The bustling commercial streets of Chinatown

TAKING A BREAK

Tha Prachan £ ❶ This is the perfect place to take a quick rest after looking around the Grand Palace. Restaurants and stalls, usually packed with market traders and students, line the path to the pier and serve anything from Chinese chicken rice and noodle soups to ice cold drinks and Thai desserts. Stroll around and pick the one that looks the busiest and best. ⓐ Next to Thammasat University and the pier Ⓝ Riverboat stop: Tha Chang

AFTER DARK

RESTAURANTS

Hippie De Bar & Restaurant £ ❷ A colourful and funky Thai house just behind D & D Inn on Khao San Road. It's always filled with locals enjoying good food, cheap drinks and music ranging from Britpop to jazz. ⓐ 46 Thanon Khao San ⓣ 02 629 3508 ⓛ 11.00–01.00 Ⓝ Riverboat stop: Phra Arthit

Kaloang Home Kitchen £ ❸ A stop at this fishhouse will take you right back to the beaches of Ko Samui. Rustic, yet cosy, it's a great place to get a simple seafood supper that you know will be fresh and tasty. ⓐ 2 Thanon Sri Ayutthaya ⓣ 02 281 9228 ⓛ 11.00–22.00 Ⓝ Riverboat stop: Thewes

May Kaidee £ ❹ Drop by this vegetarian restaurant for excellent meat-free versions of Thai favourites. If you have the time, why not take some lessons at the in-house cooking school.

ⓐ 111 Thanon Tanao ⓣ 02 281 7137 ⓦ www.maykaidee.com
ⓛ 09.00–23.00 ⓝ Riverboat stop: Phra Arthit

Ming Lee £ ⓢ Old-school Chinese food in a seriously
atmospheric eatery. If there were mafia godfathers in Bangkok,
this is where they would sup. ⓐ 29–30 Thanon Na Phra Lan
ⓛ 12.00–20.00 ⓝ Riverboat stop: Tha Chang

⬤ *You've seen the fish on the stalls, now try it for supper!*

PHRA ARTHIT ROAD
About a five-minute walk from Khao San Road is a strip
full of Thai restaurants originally opened by students from
Silpakorn University, the nearby art college. Here's where
you'll find lots of small restaurants inhabited by big
characters – it's a good way to meet a few locals. Look out
for restaurants like To-Sit and Hemlock in particular, but
there are lots of others to choose from if these are full.

BARS & CLUBS

Bangkok Bar This air-conditioned bar is a short walk from Khao
San Road on once-quiet Soi Rambuttri, an area that mirrors how
the main street was a few years ago. There is regular live music.
ⓐ 149 Soi Rambuttri ⓣ 02 629 4443 ⓛ 11.00–01.00 Ⓝ Riverboat
stop: Phra Arthit

Boh This canalside bar is a favourite among activists, bohemians
and artists, although you'd be hard-pressed to figure out why. Garish
in spots, it's still a nice place for a whisky or two. ⓐ 230 Tha Tien
ⓣ 02 622 3081 ⓛ 18.00–01.00 Ⓝ Riverboat stop: Tha Tien

Buddy Beer For years, the Khao San Road was dosshouse
central, but today it is the hip home to Thai youth and pampered
backpackers from around the world. Housed in a hip boutique
hotel, Buddy Beer is a prime example of this gentrification. You
never would have found such a clean and comfortable place to
down a drink in these parts a mere decade ago. ⓐ 265 Thanon

Khao San ☎ 02 629 4477 ⓦ www.buddygroupthailand.com
🕐 24 hrs ⓝ Riverboat stop: Phra Arthit

Café Democ This bar is a favourite among hardcore clubbers.
By day, it's a place to relax and prepare for the night ahead.
By night it dishes out some of the sparsest tunes around. You
won't be hearing any lyrics around these parts! Instead, it's all
about the beat. ⓐ 78 Thanon Ratchadamnoen Klang ☎ 02 622
2571 🕐 11.30–01.00 Tues–Sun ⓝ Riverboat stop: Tha Chang

The Club A large club on Khao San Road playing house music
in all its forms. In true Thai style you pick a table and get waiter
service for the night, usually by buying a full bottle of your
favoured spirit. Get ready for a big night out. ⓐ 123 Thanon Khao
San ☎ 02 629 1100 ⓦ www.theclubkhaosan.com 🕐 20.00–02.00

Gazebo A rooftop Moroccan-style bar with live bands and DJs to
provide the soundtrack while you puff on shisha or sip cocktails.
ⓐ 44 Thanon Chakrabong ☎ 02 629 0705 ⓦ www.gazebobkk.com
🕐 20.00–late ⓝ Riverboat stop: Phra Arthit

THEATRE
National Theatre There are plans in the works to demolish this
theatre that once housed major performances from some of the
country's top companies. Today, it is used infrequently. What
productions there tend to be on the traditional side. Check
listings for details. ⓐ Thanon Rachini ☎ 02 221 4885 🕐 Shows:
14.00–17.30 1st & 2nd weekend of the month, 17.00–19.00 last
Fri of every month ⓝ Riverboat stop: Tha Chang

KHAO SAN ROAD

Alex Garland introduced many readers to the glories and glumness of Khao San Road (Thanon Khao San) in his bestselling novel *The Beach*, but it had long been a place of transit for backpackers the world over.

In the 80s and early 90s, the Khao San Road was the residence of choice for foreigners on a really tight budget. Here, you could do your laundry after a long trek, book onward transport, find a hostel bed of varying degrees of cleanliness, transfer funds and potentially find a companion for the next leg of your journey.

The street still maintains a bit of its former buzz but, like most things made popular, is no longer the bargain it once was. Sure, you can still find cheap beds and bargain cafés, but gentrification has taken effect and boutique hotels and hip bars have now infiltrated the once-hippified alleyways.

One of the reasons for this transition is the new-found popularity the street has with Thai youth. Where before they wouldn't be caught dead wandering down its streets, a trip to the clubs and bars here is now a popular evening's entertainment.

By day, backpackers sip coffee and catch up on emails in internet cafés or flit between travel agencies to compare prices to their next dream destination. After dark, however, the street comes into its own. A party atmosphere prevails as night markets open and foreigners sit at streetside bars to sip beers and eat cheap *pad thai* or *satay*.

If you are visiting Bangkok as part of a longer stay, you'll find Khao San Road a relief due to its collection of new and second-hand bookstores offering reading material in English. Books in English can be incredibly expensive in Thailand, so you'll be thankful when you see the volume of tomes on offer. ❸ Thanon Khao San Ⓦ www.khaosanroad.com Ⓝ Riverboat stop: Phra Arthit

🔺 *Khao San Road is still a draw for travellers*

Siam Square & Sukhumvit

A hotbed of modern local culture, Siam Square is where many head to at weekends to hang out – whether shopping, gossiping in cafés, or just strolling around. You'll see Western fashion mix with Thai influences, with a healthy dash of Japanese kitsch thrown in for good measure. As well as being the central station where both BTS lines meet, this is where locals go to shop: Paragon, MBK and Siam Centre are all here. The large number of cinemas means it's also a good place to catch a movie.

Sukhumvit is a continuation of the main road and is really retail central. The area has an abundance of good hotels too. The traffic is notoriously horrendous, so don't be tempted to take a taxi. Luckily, the BTS covers most of the area.

SIGHTS & ATTRACTIONS

Baiyoke II Tower
Go to the 84th floor for sweeping views over the city below. Daytime is inspiring, but night-time truly captivates. ⓐ 22 Thanon Ratchaphrarop ⓣ 02 656 3000 ⓛ 10.30–22.00 ⓜ BTS: Phaya Thai. Admission charge

Benjakitti Park
For active travellers, this relatively new addition to the city's network of green spaces is a godsend. Packed with trails, paths, gyms and water fountains, it's a great place to get a bit of exercise. There's even a meditation centre for more contemplative activities. ⓐ Thanon Ratchadaphisek ⓣ 02 262 0810 ⓛ 05.00–20.00

🛇 BTS: Asok; MRT: Queen Sirikit Convention Centre

Benjasiri Park
Another public park for the exercise-adorer. Go here to play a game of basketball or for a dip in the admittedly tiny swimming pool. 🅐 Thanon Sukhumvit, between Soi 22 & 24 ☎ 02 262 0810 🕑 05.00–21.00 🛇 BTS: Phrom Phong

Phyathai Palace
Rama V built this royal palace in the Western style for his amusement. It's no longer used by the King, but it remains opulent – in a faded glory kind of way – nonetheless. 🅐 King Mongkutklao Hospital, 315 Thanon Ratchawithi 🛇 BTS: Victory Monument

Siam Ocean World
This aquarium – one of the world's largest – is also one of Bangkok's biggest attractions. Opened in mid-2006, it features over 35,000 fish, including massive sharks and cutesy clownfish. It has already become one of the city's major attractions. In the first two weeks of its opening, it had over 100,000 visitors. 🅐 Siam Paragon, Thanon Rama I ☎ 02 687 2000 🌐 www.siamparagon.co.th 🕑 10.00–20.00 🛇 BTS: Siam. Admission charge

Suan Pakkad Palace
Once owned by Prince and Princess Chumbhot of Nagara Svarga, this group of five teak houses has remained untouched since they died. The antiquities on display are top-notch. A peek inside feels truly special – as if you were getting a look in to

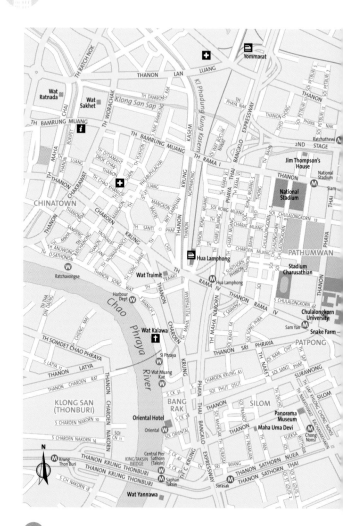

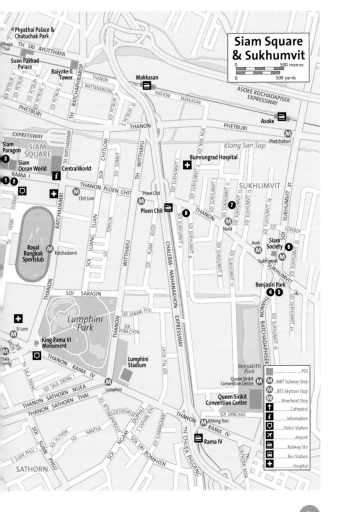

royal lifestyles and everyday living for the revered family. The lacquer collections and library are especially noteworthy. ⓐ 352 Thanon Sri Ayutthaya ⓣ 02 245 4934 ⓦ www.suanpakkad.com ⓛ 09.00–16.00 ⓝ BTS: Phaya Thai

CULTURE

Jim Thompson's House

Jim Thompson is credited with introducing the beauty of Thai silk to the world. He remains a figure of some suspicion, due to his CIA links and mysterious disappearance in Malaysia in 1967. Was he spying for the Americans or did he just stumble in the wrong direction? You decide. The mystery behind his death may never be solved, but his contribution to the Thai silk industry remains in the form of this stunning home put together from the remains of six teak houses. ⓐ 6 Soi Kasem San 2, Thanon Rama I ⓣ 02 216 7368 ⓦ www.jimthompsonhouse.com ⓛ 09.00–17.00 ⓝ BTS: National Stadium. Admission charge

Siam Society

If you are interested in the culture of Thailand's northern tribes, then this ethnographic museum is a wonderful location in which to delight your mind. The displays are well documented, covering everything from the arts to daily life. Regular lectures and workshops complete the already full schedule of events. ⓐ 131 Soi Sukhumvit 21 ⓣ 02 661 6470 ⓦ www.siam-society.org ⓛ 09.00–17.00 Tues–Sat ⓝ BTS: Asok. Admission charge

ⓞ *Jim Thompson's House is a fascinating and beautiful complex*

RETAIL THERAPY

The stretch of Thanon Rama I, on the Sukhumvit BTS line between Siam and Chit Lom stations, is department store and shopping mall central. Every major Western designer is sure to have a boutique in one of the air-conditioned temples of marble and magic that sit here. Big names like Chanel and Louis Vuitton sit alongside Thai boutiques; however, bargains are few. If the weather gets steamy, these cool capitalist ventures offer a perfect escape from the heat.

TAKING A BREAK

Lan Som Tam Nua £ ❶ Also known as Som Tam Paradise, this place serves traditional dishes from the northeast of the country such as *som tam lao* (raw and spicy papaya salad), *laab moo* (pork salad) and *khao niau* (traditional sticky rice). Most of the dishes are very spicy, so be prepared. A haven for Isaan people in Bangkok. ⓐ Siam Square, Soi 4 ❶ 02 251 4880 ❶ 10.45–21.30 ❶ BTS: Siam

Mango Tango £ ❷ If you like mango, you'll love Mango Tango. All dishes are made with sweet mango as the main ingredient. Try the Thai favourite: fresh mango with sticky rice. ⓐ Siam Square, Soi 4 ❶ 02 658 4660 ❶ 11.00–22.00 ❶ BTS: Siam

Paragon Food Hall £ ❸ For a range of good-value meals, including Chinese, Thai and Japanese specialities and tasty fruit juices, come to this food hall on the ground floor of the Siam Paragon shopping mall. ⓐ Siam Paragon, Siam Square ⓣ 02 610 9000 ⓛ 10.00–22.30 Ⓝ BTS: Siam

AFTER DARK

RESTAURANTS

Khrua Vientiane £ ❹ A true find, this one. Serving Lao specialities in a peaceful setting, Khrua Vientiane is a great place for a country-style meal complete with dancers and musicians – and not of the cheesy strolling violin sort. Good if you're looking for something cheap, yet atmospheric. ⓐ 8 Soi Sukhumvit 36 ⓣ 02 258 6171 ⓦ www.vientiane-kitchen.com ⓛ 12.00–00.00 Ⓝ BTS: Thong Lo

Govinda ££ ❺ Vegetarian food is easy to come by in Bangkok, but this Italian restaurant specialising in meat-free dishes makes a nice change of pace from the constant supply of spring rolls. ⓐ 6/5–6 Soi Sukhumvit 22 ⓣ 02 663 4970 ⓦ www.nutritionhouse.co.th ⓛ 11.30–15.00, 18.00–00.00 Mon, Wed–Sun Ⓝ BTS: Phrom Phong

Minibar Royale ££ ❻ New York meets Paris in this unusual little restaurant. An imaginative menu complements a champagne-based cocktail list and it is very popular with locals so make sure you book if you want to try it out. ⓐ 37/7 Citadines Bangkok, Sukhumvit 23 ⓣ 02 261 5533 ⓦ www.minibarroyale.com ⓛ 10.30–00.00 Ⓝ BTS: Asok; MRT: Sukhumvit

Bed Supperclub £££ ❼ The whole concept of eating in bed may be a bit old hat, but it remains just as hip as it ever was here in Bangkok. Interiors are chic; the diners are even chicer. The three-course set menu may not be the best you've ever had, but it is sure to please. After dinner, the bar heats up and the flirting kicks into overdrive. ⓐ 26 Soi Sukhumvit 11 ⓣ 02 651 3537 ⓦ www.bedsupperclub.com ⓛ 19.30–02.00 ⓝ BTS: Nana

New York Steakhouse £££ ❽ If you're sick of the idea of another bowl of *pad thai* and require a venue that will impress, then this is the eatery to make a reservation at. Prime cuts of beef are served in a very masculine atmosphere resembling a Pall Mall private club. It's expensive, but worth it if you need to close that deal. ⓐ J W Marriott Hotel, 4 Soi Sukhumvit 2 ⓣ 02 656 7700 ⓛ 18.00–23.00 ⓝ BTS: Nana

BARS & CLUBS
Cheap Charlies A favourite of expats living in Bangkok, this bar is the easiest place to make new friends. It's outside – actually on the street - and Sathit, the owner and barman, is hidden behind a collection of strange and unusual artefacts. It's the sort of place that could only exist in Bangkok and has to be seen to be believed. There are lots of great eateries around it, serving a choice of Indian, Mexican and Spanish food. ⓐ Soi Sukhumvit 11 ⓛ 18.00–01.00 Mon–Sat ⓝ BTS: Nana

Hard Rock Café This may be a well-known international chain bar and restaurant, but it's not here to cater just for tourists: the locals love it. During the day it's great for a meal if you have

⬥ *Siam Paragon is one of Bangkok's best shopping malls*

fussy kids, and by night things hot up with the appearance of a young, trendy crowd. ⓐ Siam Square, Soi 11 ⓣ 02 251 0797 ⓛ 11.00–01.00 Ⓝ BTS: Siam

Q Bar Probably Bangkok's hippest nightclub (at least for now), this sleek and chic venue pulls in the fantastic and fabulous of the city. Drinks are expensive for this part of the world, but you're paying to be surrounded by the beautiful people. ⓐ 34 Soi Sukhumvit 11 ⓣ 02 252 3274 ⓦ www.qbarbangkok.com ⓛ 20.00–02.00 Ⓝ BTS: Nana

CINEMAS & THEATRES

Company of Performing Artists The performance venue for Thailand's most creative dance company, which fuses traditional movements, classical ballet and contemporary techniques. ⓐ 6th Floor, Central World, Zone Central Court ⓣ 02 613 1670 ⓦ www.dance-centre.com Ⓝ BTS: Siam

CINEMA SCENE
Excellent cinemas can be found in this area of central Bangkok and the facilities are second to none. Almost all big Hollywood movies are shown, along with many films belonging to the burgeoning home-grown scene – some translated into English. The best ways to find out what's on where are to check the *Bangkok Post* or click on ⓦ www.movieseer.com, which gives full listings of all cinemas.

Mambo Drag queens are revered in Thailand for their skill and beauty. Known as *kathoey*, these performers put on the glitz every night to a crowd of appreciative locals. ⓐ Washington Theatre, 496 Thanon Sukhumvit ⓣ 02 259 5715 ⓛ 10.00–18.00, performances: 20.30, 22.00 ⓝ BTS: Phrom Phong

Siam Niramit With a capacity of over 2,000 seats, this theatre is one of the world's largest. Catch the kitsch Thai cultural show that is performed here every night if you enjoy fusions of folklore and glitz. ⓐ Ratchada Grand Theatre, 19 Thanon Tiamruammit ⓣ 02 533 1152 ⓦ www.siamniramit.com ⓛ Performances nightly at 19.30 ⓝ MRT: Thailand Cultural Centre

Silom & Thonburi

Silom and nearby Sathorn are the heart of Bangkok's business district and run from the centre of the city to the river and Chinatown.

The area begins at the southern edge of Lumphini Park. As you move down Silom Road you'll meet towering office blocks interspersed with shopping complexes and market stalls – the locals really do take every opportunity to shop. Silom is a hive of activity day or night, as when the office workers have gone, Patpong night market comes alive. Patpong is as well known for its raunchy nightlife as for its shopping opportunities (see page 33). A Thai boxing stadium is close by at the Suan Lum Night Bazaar, so there is plenty to keep you busy. Silom is also serviced by both the MRT and BTS, making it a good place to base yourself.

Head to Saphan Taksin on the BTS line to find the starting point for river cruises and the crossing into sleepy Thonburi. High-rises suddenly stop as you cross the river, although that may all be about to change as the BTS and property developers extend their reach.

Thonburi was the site of the original royal palaces in the area and was briefly the centre of government before Rama I decided to build the current Grand Palace. Many of the old buildings from that period still remain, with Wat Arun being the highlight.

SIGHTS & ATTRACTIONS

Lumphini Park

Bangkok's favourite public park is this vast network of lawns

◆ *Floral offerings at a temple in Thonburi*

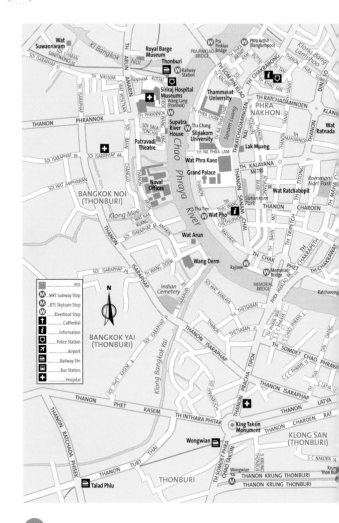

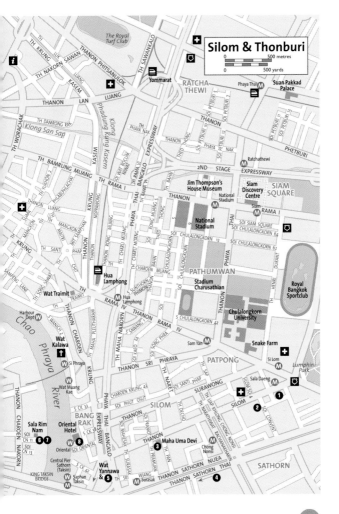

MESSING ABOUT ON THE RIVER

There is so much to see and do along the river that you'd be well advised to take a river cruise. The Chao Phraya Express Boats offer a hop-on, hop-off river cruise for tourists, starting at either Sathorn pier by King Taksin Bridge or Phra Arthit pier next to Khao San Road. The boats depart on the hour and half hour from each pier, between 09.30 and 17.00.

The boat stops at many piers along the route, with some of the highlights being:

- Tha Tien: An unmissable stop. As you disembark you'll see the impressive Wat Arun (Temple of Dawn) on the opposite side of the river (to get there you'll need to switch boats). Staying on your own side of the river, meander through the riverside stalls to get to Wat Pho, which features both the reclining Buddha and also a famous massage school. The surrounding market is just as interesting, for browsing as well as buying, and the Grand Palace is also a stone's throw away.
- Wang Lang: This busy pier serves as the gateway for the huge Siriraj Hospital Museums (see page 98). The Patravadi Theatre is nearby, offering classic and folk Thai performances, as is Supatra River House.
- Phra Arthit: Guarding Phra Arthit road and surrounding areas is the Phra Sumane Fort, one of only two forts that survive from the beginning of Bangkok's history around 1782. At one time there were 14 forts defending

the city from a river attack.
- The Oriental hotel (see page 40): Stop here for tea and watch the river traffic pass by.
- Si Phraya: Famous for arts and antiques, the River City shopping complex is found here.

and paths located in the heart of the city. At dawn, the park comes alive with strollers, exercisers and *t'ai chi* practitioners. You can even see boxers practising the martial arts sport of *Muay Thai*, or enjoy a picnic by the live stages on Sunday afternoons. Be sure to avoid the place after dark, when this family-focused centre for fun becomes a much less desirable location.
ⓐ 192 Thanon Rama IV ① 02 252 7006 ⓛ 04.30–21.00
Ⓝ BTS: Sala Daeng; MRT: Si Lom

Maha Uma Devi

Hindus consider this shrine the most important in Bangkok. A centre of activity during important festivals such as Diwali, it is covered in depictions of Hindu gods and goddesses – particularly of Shiva's consort, after whom the temple is named. ⓐ 2 Thanon Pan ① 02 238 4007 ⓛ 06.00–20.00 Sat–Thur, 06.00–21.00 Fri Ⓝ BTS: Surasak

Snake Farm

This is not a theme park but an actual working clinic conducting research on and creating antivenom for the six snake species documented as deadly in Thailand. It's only of interest to visitors when the handlers are scheduled to milk the snakes – so check times in advance. ❸ Queen Saovabha Memorial Institute, 1871 Thanon Rama IV ❶ 02 252 0161 ❷ 08.30–16.30 Mon–Fri, 08.30–12.00 Sat & Sun ❷ BTS: Sala Daeng. Admission charge

⬤ *Savour the atmosphere at Wat Arun*

Wang Derm

Formerly an important royal palace, this compound was
a favourite of King Taksin and saw the birth of three future
kings. It was given to the Royal Navy during the rule of Rama V;
however, there were strict conditions that had to be followed,
including the maintenance of the throne room, which you can
see today. All visits must be booked and confirmed in advance.
ⓐ Thai Royal Navy Headquarters, 2 Phra Ratcha Wang Derm,
Thanon Arun Amarin ⓣ 02 475 4117 ⓦ www.wangdermpalace.com
ⓛ 08.30–16.00 Ⓝ Riverboat stop: Tha Tien, then catch boat
across river

Wat Arun (Temple of the Dawn)

Wat Arun is a notable landmark primarily due to its large *prang*
(spire), which stands 81 m (266 ft) high. From a distance it looks
like a beehive or corncob. The views from the top are stunning –
unfortunately, you can't enjoy them anymore, since a tourist fell
off in 1998. Try to time your visit to end just before sunset, as
the view of Wat Arun from the other side of the river is superb.
ⓐ Thanon Arun Amarin ⓣ 02 891 1149 ⓦ www.watarun.org
ⓛ 07.00–18.00 Ⓝ Riverboat stop: Tha Tien, then catch boat
across river. Admission charge

Wat Suwannaram

Beautiful proportions and enchanting interior murals are what
make this temple so special. You'll often see students in the
courtyards attempting to sketch the works as practice for their
own artistic feats. ⓐ 33 Soi Charan Sanitwong 32 ⓣ 02 433 8045
ⓛ 08.30–16.30 Ⓝ Riverboat stop: Railway Station

Wat Yannawa

What makes this temple unique is the fact that it looks
like a Chinese junk. This wasn't the original design, however,
but merely an addition created during the reign of Rama III.
Interesting to glance at in passing, but not worth going well out
of your way to see. ⓐ 1648 Thanon Charoen Krung ⓣ 02 211 9317
ⓛ 05.00–21.00 ⓝ BTS: Saphan Taksin

CULTURE

Royal Barge Museum

Like the royal carriages owned by the British royal family, the
royal barges instil a sense of awe in onlookers when they pass
by on their way to special functions. Beautiful to look at due
to their sleek lines and the craftsmanship that goes into their
construction, they are even more inspiring once you examine
the ancient reasoning that goes behind the creation of each
one. Many, including the *Suphannahongse* (Golden Swan),
were constructed from a single log, and required a minimum
of 50 men to row. ⓐ 80/1 Rimklong Bangkok Noi, Thanon Arun
Amarin ⓣ 02 424 0004 ⓛ 09.00–17.00 ⓝ Riverboat stop: Pra
Pinklao Bridge. Admission charge

Siriraj Hospital Museums

Definitely not for the fainthearted, this collection of six
museums chronicles the human body. Exhibits include organs,
deformed stillbirths, Siamese twin bones, obscure embryos and
much more. The museum was intended as an educational tool
for medical students, but tends to draw visitors with a taste for

the bizarre. ⓐ Thanon Phrannok ❶ 02 419 7000 ❷ 08.30–16.30
Ⓝ Riverboat stop: Wang Lang

RETAIL THERAPY

Thonburi isn't known for its markets or shopping options;
however, it is the gateway to the traditional floating markets

● *The floating markets are one of Bangkok's quintessential images*

located to the west of the city. Considered the district of canals, the region to the west of Thonburi is the best place to head for if you want to visit bustling markets that exist right on the ancient *klongs* (canals). As river traffic has historically been so important in Thailand, merchants have developed innovative ways to help sell their wares.

Floating markets are a kind of drive-through convenience store with almost everything you might need for a long journey up the river available for purchase. Tourists have also been taken into account, with many a tout selling souvenirs and trinkets.

Go early if you want to see the action the way Thais see it, as many coachloads destroy the views from around 09.00 onwards. The most famous of the lot is at Damnoen Saduak; however, this is also the most touristy. If you can, try to go further west to the markets at Tha Kha, Lam Phya or Don Wai.

TAKING A BREAK

Nooddi £ ❶ Almost like a food stall set inside a restaurant, Nooddi is known for one thing – noodles. Thai, Chinese, Japanese, Italian, Vietnamese: you'll find them all here at pocket-friendly prices. Great place for a quick snack. ⓐ Sala Daeng Station, Silom ❶ 02 658 4481 ⓦ www.nooddithai.com ⓛ 11.00–22.00 ⓝ BTS: Sala Daeng

Molly Malones ££ ❷ You can't go far in the world these days without meeting an Irish pub, but Molly's is perfectly placed to take the strain off after a day of pounding the streets. Good food and friendly staff make this a welcome stopping point. ⓐ Soi

Convent, Silom ☏ 02 266 7160 ⓦ www.mollymalonesbangkok.com
🕐 09.00–01.00 Ⓝ BTS: Sala Daeng

AFTER DARK

RESTAURANTS

Café De Laos £ ❸ Hidden between Silom and Sathorn roads is this teakwood colonial-style house which serves up delicious Northeast Thai food. You can sit inside or out in the garden, and can even accompany the meal with a bottle of Thai whisky (to be drunk with soda, cola, or a mix of both). This is food from the country so don't shirk if you see frog or even snake on the menu.
ⓐ Soi Silom 19, Silom ☏ 02 635 2338 ⓦ www.cafedelaos.com
🕐 11.00–14.00, 17.00–22.00 Ⓝ BTS: Surasak

Blue Elephant ££ ❹ A meal at this Thai restaurant and cooking school is a treat: what makes it extra special are the excellent cooking courses offered every day (see page 29). Who knows, what you eat today might become your staple recipe tomorrow.
ⓐ 233 Thanon Sathorn Tai ☏ 02 673 9353 ⓦ www.blueelephant.com
🕐 11.30–14.30, 18.30–22.00 Ⓝ BTS: Surasak

River Bar Café ££ ❺ Unlike other riverside eateries, this café features designer interiors – no simple cushions and cheap Thai silks here. Go for unfussy, yet stylish seafood dishes in a fashionable location. It lies south of the Saphan Taksin riverboat stop, off Thanon Charoen Krung ⓐ 405/1 Soi Chao Phraya Siam, Thanon Ratchawithi ☏ 02 879 1748 ⓦ www.riverbar.com 🕐 17.00–02.00
Ⓝ Riverboat stop: Saphan Taksin

Jester's £££ ❽ If you're tired of Thai food and want a blowout meal that will bring you back into the realm of international fusion flavour, then make Jester's your destination of choice. Not only will the river views inspire you, you'll also love the intriguing flavours that draw from every culinary tradition around the world. ⓐ 1st Floor, Peninsula Hotel, 333 Thanon Charoen Nakorn ⓣ 02 861 2888 ⓦ www.peninsula.com ⓛ 18.00–22.30 Tues–Sun (bar open until 00.00) Ⓝ BTS: Saphan Taksin, then catch shuttle boat

Mei Jiang £££ ❼ The Peninsula Hotel rivals the Oriental in terms of sheer opulence – and this restaurant is one of its showpieces. Cantonese cuisine in a classically luxurious setting is what's on offer. Expect a large bill. ⓐ 1st Floor, Peninsula Hotel, 333 Thanon Charoen Nakorn ⓣ 02 861 2888 ⓦ www.peninsula.com ⓛ 11.30–14.30, 18.00–22.30 Ⓝ BTS: Saphan Taksin, then catch shuttle boat

Le Normandie £££ ❾ If you can't afford a night at the Oriental, then a meal here is the next best thing. Probably Bangkok's most famous restaurant, this dining room feels like a slice out of Paris. You arguably wouldn't find better French cuisine even if you were eating on the Champs-Elysées itself. Jackets and ties are compulsory. ⓐ 5th Floor, Oriental Hotel, 48 Oriental Avenue, off Thanon Charoen Krung ⓣ 02 659 9000 ⓦ www.mandarinoriental.com ⓛ 12.00–14.00, 19.00–22.30 Ⓝ Riverboat stop: Oriental

BARS & CLUBS
Sky Bar Views to die for from this rooftop bar on the 63rd floor

of the Lebua State Tower. It's perfect for a sunset drink – and worth staying to see the city light up at night. It's not cheap, but definitely worth it. Smart casual attire, i.e. trousers are essential and flip-flops a no-no. ⓐ State Tower, 1055 Thanon Silom ⓣ 02 624 9999 ⓦ http://bangkok.lebua.com ⓛ 18.00–01.00 ⓝ BTS: Saphan Taksin

Tapas Bangkok clubs come and go but Tapas has outlived most. Three intimate floors play groovy party music to a mix of locals and expats with live percussionists. If you don't want to dance there is a small outside terrace which is great for watching the surrounding nightlife. ⓐ Silom Soi 4, Silom ⓣ 02 234 4737 ⓦ www.tapasroom.net ⓛ 20.00–02.00 ⓝ BTS: Sala Daeng

Vertigo Like the Sky Bar, this bar on the 61st floor of the Banyan Tree hotel has superb views over the city. Again, it's not cheap, but it's a breathtaking experience. Dress smartly. ⓐ 21/100 Thanon Sathorn Tai, Sathorn ⓣ 02 679 1200 ⓦ www.banyantree.com ⓛ 18.30–23.00 ⓝ BTS: Sala Daeng then 10 min walk; MRT: Lumphini

THEATRE

Patravadi Theatre Independent theatre and dance find fans at this open-air complex that has been an institution with the bohemian set since it opened in 1992. Worth checking out to see what art is bubbling up from the underground. ⓐ 69/1 Soi Wat Rakhang, Thanon Arun Amarin ⓣ 02 412 7287 ⓛ Box office: 08.30–18.00. Performances between 19.30 & 21.00 ⓦ www.patravaditheatre.com ⓝ Riverboat stop: Wang Lang

Sala Rim Nam When the Oriental Hotel wants to do something, you can guarantee they'll do it right – and this theatre offering Thai dance performance is no exception. The hall itself is enchanting, featuring the finest bronzes, polished teak and a blissful riverside setting. Performers come from the Bangkok Department of Fine Arts and showcase both folk and classical dance varieties. Reservations recommended. ⓐ Oriental Hotel, 48 Oriental Avenue, off Thanon Charoen Krung ⓣ 02 437 2918 ⓛ 19.00–22.00. Performances nightly at 20.30 Ⓝ Riverboat stop: Oriental

Supatra River House Enjoy traditional Thai dance and a fantastic meal at this dinner theatre that blows the competition away. Be sure to get there early, as some of the seats do not have a good view of the stage. Ferry transfers can be arranged by the theatre – call in advance for a reservation ⓐ 266 Soi Wat Rakhang, Thanon Arun Amarin ⓣ 02 411 0305 ⓦ www.supatrariverhouse.net ⓛ 20.30 Fri & Sat Ⓝ Riverboat stop: Wang Lang

▶ *The famous bridge on the River Kwai*

OUT OF TOWN
trips

Ayutthaya

A visit to the UNESCO World Heritage Site of Ayutthaya is truly one of the highlights of any visit to Bangkok. As the capital of the Kingdom of Siam from 1350 to 1760, Ayutthaya must have been a real marvel during its heyday. Today, attacks by the Burmese and a lack of upkeep over the centuries have given the area the feeling of a 'lost town' that has only recently been discovered.

Over 33 kings called Ayutthaya home, with its peak occurring in the 18th century, when the region boasted three palaces and over 400 temples. A 15-month siege by the Burmese in 1767 ended the town's Golden Age and resulted in its almost complete destruction (see page 16).

Tourism Authority of Thailand ⓐ Thanon Si Sanphet
ⓘ 03 532 2730 ⓦ www.tourismthailand.org

GETTING THERE

Fifteen trains a day make the trip from Bangkok's Hua Lamphong Station. Express trains are your best bet as they offer air-conditioned comfort. The journey time is about 90 minutes. Alternatively, buses depart every 20 minutes from Bangkok's Northern & Northeastern Bus Terminal.

A popular choice for tourists is to include a visit to Ayutthaya as part of an all-day river cruise. **River Sun Cruises** (ⓘ 02 673 0966 ⓦ www.thai-tour.com) is one of the better operators. Tours depart from the River City Pier.

⬥ *The Summer Palace Temple in the royal gardens at Ayutthaya*

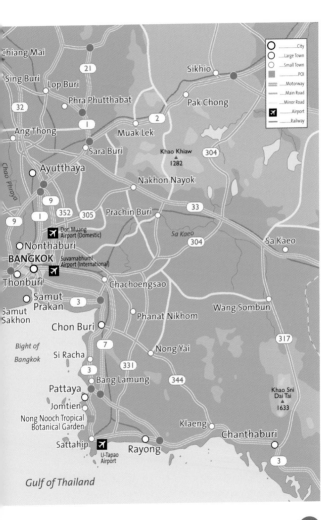

SIGHTS & ATTRACTIONS

Ancient Palace

Destroyed by the Burmese in 1767, this palace is still of interest, as its foundations remain. You can get an idea of what the opulence and grandeur must have been like simply by wandering the remains of its walls and base. ⓐ Northwest section of old city ⓛ 08.00–18.00

Wat Chai Wattanaram

Probably the most intact temple in Ayutthaya, this *wat* needs a certain determination to visit. Located across the river in the southwest of the city, you will need to find a *tuk-tuk* or rent a bike to reach the complex. Once there, it's a steep climb up a series of steps – but the view over the surrounding countryside more than makes up for it. ⓐ Southwest section of old city ⓣ 03 524 2501 ⓛ 08.30–16.30. Admission charge

Wat Na Phra Mane

As one of the few temples to survive the wrath of the Burmese, this *wat* remains beautifully intact. The highlight to any visit is the magnificently carved black stone Buddha that dates back to the Dvaravati period (6th to 11th century). ⓐ North of Ancient Palace ⓛ 08.30–16.30. Admission charge

Wat Phra Mongkol Bopit

Like a big fish in a small pond, Thailand's largest seated bronze Buddha seems to take up every inch of space in this compact *wat*. The Buddha image was created in the 17th century to

WAT MAHATHAT

Wat Mahathat feels a bit like something out of *Raiders of the Lost Ark*. Ruined Buddhas mix with crumbling *stupas* (dome-shaped monuments) in what must once have been Ayutthaya's finest temple. Built from 1374 onwards, it is the most atmospheric of all the ruins on site and a popular place from which to enjoy the sunset. ⓐ Thanon Sikhun ⓘ 03 524 2501 ⓛ 08.00–18.00. Admission charge

honour Naresuan, the brother of the King, who was famous for winning great battles against the ever-threatening Burmese. ⓐ South of Ancient Palace ⓛ 08.30–16.30. Admission charge

Wat Phra Sri Sanphet

This temple was originally the private chapel of the King, but was destroyed in 1767 when the attacking Burmese attempted to melt the gold of the Buddha image it contained. Fire swept the building, destroying its precious interiors. What you see today is actually a reconstruction. ⓐ South of Ancient Palace ⓘ 03 524 2501 ⓛ 07.00–18.30. Admission charge

Wat Yai Chai Mongkon

You can't miss this *wat* due to its massive gold *chedi* (*stupa*) (bell-shaped tower). Founded in the 14th century, the temple is one of the oldest and most beautiful in the city. The numerous Buddhas surrounding the *chedi* are actually recent additions. ⓐ Northwest of train station ⓛ 08.00–18.00. Admission charge

◔ *The temple at Wat Phra Sri Sanphet*

CULTURE

Ayutthaya Historical Culture Centre
Built to assist scholars and students, this centre features miniature exhibits that showcase what areas of the city may have looked like during its peak years of importance, in addition to artefacts that hark back to the golden years in question.
ⓐ Thanon Rojana ⓣ 03 524 5124 ⓛ 09.00–16.30 Mon–Fri, 09.00–17.00 Sat & Sun. Admission charge

Chandra Kasem Palace
Built for King Naresuan in the late 16th century, this palace is now a branch of the National Museum and currently holds a collection of artefacts discovered in the region that date back to between the 13th and 17th centuries. ⓐ Northeast section of old city ⓛ 09.00–12.00, 13.00–16.00 Wed–Sun. Admission charge

Chao Sam Phraya National Museum
As the second-largest museum in Thailand, the Chao Sam Phraya is an absolute must. Packed with treasures, it hosts an impressive collection of Buddhas and religious objects.
ⓐ Thanon Rojana ⓣ 03 524 1587 ⓛ 09.00–16.00 Wed–Sun. Admission charge

RETAIL THERAPY

Night Market
Thai fruits and vegetables, yummy meals and cheap trinkets can all be picked up at this atmospheric market that is sure to add

a touch of spice to any visit. A second market called the 'New Night Market' has recently opened south of Wat Mahathat to help alleviate overcrowding. ⓐ Northeast of town near the pier ⓛ 20.00–late

TAKING A BREAK

Siam Restaurant £ Cool down at this air-conditioned Thai eatery located conveniently across the street from Wat Mahathat. It's the best place to head for when you need a break from temple hopping. ⓐ 11/3 Thanon Pratuchai ⓣ 03 521 1070 ⓛ 10.00–22.00

AFTER DARK

RESTAURANTS

Pae Krung Kao £ Every traveller who comes to Thailand has a picture of what the perfect restaurant should look like, and this is it. Situated on a series of floating piers, this casual restaurant features acoustic musicians playing 60s standards, fantastic stir-frys and views of the *klongs* as long-tails pass you by. Sheer bliss. ⓐ 4 Moo 2, Thanon U-Thong ⓣ 03 524 1555 ⓛ 09.00–21.00

Ruen Rub Rong £–££ Another riverside eatery, this one features a dinner-cruise option. Ring to check departure times. ⓐ 13/1–2 Thanon U-Thong ⓣ 03 524 3090 ⓛ 10.00–22.00

BARS & CLUBS

Ayutthaya isn't really known as a party town. Instead, pull up a chair at one of the riverside eateries and cool down with a bottle of local beer. A night of clubbing simply won't be on the cards.

ACCOMMODATION

Baan Suan Guest House £ A friendly and affordable family-run guesthouse with an amazing in-house kitchen. ⓐ 23/1 Thanon Chakrapat ⓣ 03 524 2394 ⓦ www.baansuanguesthouse.com

Bann Kun Pra £ As long as you don't try to check in during the hot season, this property is the best in town for the price. The converted teak house is incredibly romantic, even if the actual interiors are somewhat countrified. A lack of air conditioning is the only major drawback. Don't go expecting any luxury. ⓐ 48 Moo Thanon U-Thong ⓣ 03 524 1978 ⓦ www.bannkunpra.com

Krungsri River Hotel ££ If the lobby impresses you, then you might be slightly disappointed once you see the large, yet bland rooms. Expect lots of function and little form. You'll need to take the complimentary shuttle to see the major sights. ⓐ 7/2 Thanon Rojana ⓣ 03 524 4333 ⓦ www.krungsririverhotel.com

Kanchanaburi & the Bridge on the River Kwai

Made famous in the 1957 David Lean film of the same name, the Bridge on the River Kwai is located approximately 5 km (3 miles) north of the town of Kanchanaburi – a busy provincial city that is capital of Kanchanaburi province.

The plot of the movie, which was based on a French novel by author Pierre Boulle, differs hugely from the actual truth behind the bridge's construction. While the film depicts a commando-led mission to explode the structure, the bridge wasn't destroyed until Allied bombs hit it two years after its completion.

The Japanese built the bridge in order to link the existing Thai and Burmese railway lines, thereby creating a permanent

▲ *Discover the truth behind the famous bridge on the River Kwai*

route between Bangkok and Rangoon in order to support Japanese occupation of Southeast Asia. Over 110,000 people died during its construction due to malnourishment and disease, including over 100,000 indentured Asian labourers and 12,000 Allied prisoners of war.

The character of Nicholson depicted in the film caused much controversy among soldiers who worked on the bridge's construction, with many feeling it insulted the memory of Philip Toosey, the actual Lieutenant Colonel who led the prisoners during the construction period. Pierre Boulle himself admitted that no such character ever existed. Instead, he based Nicholson on French collaborators who worked with the Japanese during his time in Thai prisoner of war camps.

In reality, two bridges were built by labourers – one temporary wooden structure and a permanent steel and concrete span that remains in use today.

GETTING THERE

Take the train from either Thonburi or Hua Lamphong station to Kanchanaburi. Trains leave frequently throughout the day; however, the departure at 06.30 at weekends is the most convenient. The trip takes around three hours. Coaches also make the journey, departing from the Southern Bus Terminal every 20 minutes between 05.00 and 22.30.

TAKING A BREAK

Head to the riverside and the bars that line Thanon Song Kwae

THE COSTS OF WAR

For a grim reminder of the costs of war, head to the nearby Kanchanaburi War Cemetery, which is home to the bodies of over 7,000 PoWs. Located approximately 1.5 km (1 mile) from the train station, it is open every day from 08.30 to 18.00. Graves are marked and ordered by country.

Two museums also tell the story of the PoWs – the Thailand–Burma Railway Centre and Jeath War Museum. Both chronicle the experiences faced by the prisoners, including photos, maps, films and personal histories. The museums are open from 08.30 to 16.30.

for tasty morsels and inspiring views. All of the eateries are of similar quality, so just pull up a chair and sit yourself down for an evening of pleasure for your stomach.

ACCOMMODATION

Felix River Kwai Resort £ Comfortable resort offering the basics, including much-needed air conditioning. ⓐ 9/1 Moo 3 Tambon, Kanchanaburi ⓣ 03 455 1000 ⓦ www.felixriverkwai.co.th

Jungle Raft Resort £ If you're an adventurous type, check into one of the floating river rafts that make up this resort complex. Avoid staying here during the hot and humid season, as the mozzie problem can get severe. ⓐ Lam Khao Ngu ⓣ 02 642 5497 ⓦ www.riverkwaijunglerafts.com

Pattaya

A seaside resort for Bangkok's weekend-break set, Pattaya began its life as a humble fishing village, exploding into the glittering getaway it now is during the Vietnam War. American GIs on R&R breaks were beckoned to this village of girlie bars and cheap hotels, leaving heaps of Western dollars in their wake. And as the money poured in, so did the girls – desperate for cash or the dream of a life in the West. The soldiers may no longer be here, but the prostitutes, shocking sex shows and cheap bars remain. Family entertainment, it isn't.

One beach further south, however, is Jomtien – a beautiful and extremely family-friendly stretch of sand that seems a world away from the problems of Pattaya. Here you can find great resort deals that would cost hundreds of pounds a night in other locations such as the Costa del Sol or Florida. Most Thai holidaymakers choose Jomtien as their base by day and Pattaya as their home by night; thus combining the best of both worlds. Pattaya really does look a lot better when the sun has gone down and the neon is switched on to bathe you in its multi-coloured glow.

Child sex tourism is a real problem in Pattaya, and there are regular reports of Western men being arrested and/or deported by Thai police after being caught with under-age sex workers – both male and female. Please be aware at all times of any scams you might become subject to, as it is not unknown for local police forces to collaborate with prostitution rings in order to boost their arrest records.

Tourism Authority of Thailand ⓐ 609 Thanon Phra Tamnak ⓣ 03 842 8750

GETTING THERE

Take the daily train from Bangkok's Hua Lamphong Station
which leaves every day at 06.55 (check timetables to confirm).
The trip takes five hours in total but provides nice views of the
countryside and will give you a chance to meet the locals.
Coaches – both private and public – depart from the Eastern
Bus Terminal and depart about every 30 minutes. A ride in an
air-conditioned public bus will cost you about B90.

Taxis are more than happy to take you to Pattaya. Negotiate
your fare in advance and expect to pay about B1,250.

SIGHTS & ATTRACTIONS

Mini Siam

See all the famous sights of Thailand in miniature and give
yourself a Gulliver-sized ego when you stand above the waist-

● *South of Pattaya is the beautiful beach at Jomtien*

high Grand Palace. ❷ 387 Moo, 6 Thanon Sukhumvit, North Pattaya City ❶ 03 872 7333 ⓦ www.minisiam.com ⏰ 07.00–22.00. Admission charge

Nong Nooch Tropical Botanical Garden

Of all the tourist attractions in Pattaya, this is one of the best, even though it's located 18 km (11 miles) outside the city limits. Options include Thai dancing performances, elephant rides, Thai boxing matches, music and introductions to Thai cultural traditions. Shuttles depart from all major Pattaya and Jomtien properties at 08.30 or 13.15 every day. Return trips can also be arranged. Call the park in advance to book space. ❶ 03 842 9321 ⓦ www.nongnoochtropicalgarden.com. Admission charge

Pattaya Elephant Village

If you disagree with animal circus acts, then this park may not be for you. Kids, however, may enjoy the performing elephants and elephant-back rides. Half-hour jungle treks on elephant

back are also available. ⓐ Nern Plub Wan Road, off Sukhumvit Road, km 145 ⓦ www.elephant-village-pattaya.com ⓛ Shows: 14.30; rides: 09.00, 10.30, 12.30, 16.30

Pattaya Go-Kart

Here you can zoom around the 400 m (437 yard) track in a variety of speedy vehicles. It's suitable for children aged eight and up and prices vary according to the quality of your desired kart. It's located next to Mini Siam and the two together make a full day out for a family. ⓐ 8 Thanon Sukhumvit ⓣ 03 842 2044 ⓛ 09.30–18.30. Admission charge

Phoenix Golf Club

Well-maintained golf club popular with both the expat community and Bangkok's middle-class holidaymakers. ⓐ Thanon Sukhumvit ⓣ 03 823 9391 ⓛ 07.00–18.00. Admission charge

Ripley's Believe It or Not Museum

The world's most bizarre exhibits are packed into one curious collection in this museum, which has branches all across the US and UK. Lacking in anything educational, it's more for the voyeur in all of us. For something a little wilder, go next door to the Motion Master simulation ride. ⓐ 3rd Floor, Royal Garden Plaza, 218 Thanon Beach Road ⓣ 03 871 0294 ⓦ www.ripleys.com ⓛ 10.00–00.00. Admission charge

Sanctuary of Truth

You'll see plenty of signs advertising this watershow park around town. Be advised that the happy dolphins in the ads are far from thrilled when you see them up close. Go if you want to use the horse-riding trails and the speedboat thrill shows – just be warned that our friendly fellow mammals may not be treated the way they should. **ⓐ** 206/2 Soi Naklua 12 **ⓣ** 03 836 7229 **ⓦ** www.sanctuaryoftruth.com **ⓛ** 10.00–20.00. Admission charge

CULTURE

Culture? In Pattaya? You must be joking. This town focuses on pleasure and not education. If you're looking for museums and galleries, then you might want to look elsewhere.

RETAIL THERAPY

Shopping in Pattaya is restricted to souvenir shops and cheap trinkets. If you're looking for carved wooden elephants and cheap silk shirts, then you'll be in luck. Otherwise, leave the big purchases to Bangkok.

TAKING A BREAK

PIC Kitchen £ This collection of air-conditioned and open-air teak pavilions is a great place for a casual lunch on a hot day. Let fragrant breezes cool you as you tuck into some of Pattaya's finest and freshest seafood dishes. As an added plus, a live band plays every evening from 19.00. **ⓐ** Soi 5, Pattaya 2nd Road **ⓣ** 03 842 8374 **ⓛ** 08.00–00.00

THE HAPPY HOOKERS?

Whether or not you agree with the practice of prostitution, it's hard to avoid evidence of this booming industry in Pattaya. Most prostitutes in the city ply their trade for Thais; however, there are many that focus on Westerners as a source for potential matrimonial escape. Many of the girls on offer hail from the extremely rural and poverty-stricken farmlands of Isaan. For them, prostitution is a choice between life and death.

Pattaya also boasts a huge gay scene, with rent boys catering to the needs of holidaying homosexuals. The gay village is located on Pattayaland Soi 3 (otherwise known as 'Boys Town'). Venues range from casual gay cafés to full-on showbars, complete with rentable escorts and live sex shows.

Thais and Westerners patrol Pattaya and think nothing of popping into sex-themed venues as a form of entertainment. You will see lone men, young couples and grannies pop in to witness the excitement. Whether you're one of them or decide to avoid the places altogether, you should come armed with some key knowledge.

If you see the exploitation of a minor, please report it to the police. Thailand can only battle the practice of under-age exploitation with your help. If you do decide to enter a showbar, keep watch on your drinks at all times as druggings have been known. Also, ask about drink prices and door fees in advance, or you may be stung with a massive bill at the end of your evening. Finally, condoms are an absolute must. AIDS is prevalent in Thailand and you should practise safe sex at all times.

For further information about the prostitution industry in Thailand, legalities, and what you can do to assist the status of women in the country, contact the **National Council of Women in Thailand** (ⓐ Baan Manangkasila, 514 Thanon Lan Luang, Bangkok ① 02 281 0081 Ⓦ www.thaiwomen.or.th ⓛ 08.30–16.30 Mon–Fri).

● *Pattaya is home to some of Thailand's ladyboys*

AFTER DARK

RESTAURANTS

Shere E Punjab £–££ Head here for authentic northern Indian cuisine in an intimate setting. Pull up a chair at one of the candlelit outdoor tables or enjoy the air-conditioned comfort inside the main restaurant. ⓐ 216 Soi 11, Thanon Beach ⓣ 03 842 0158 ⓛ 12.00–01.00

Henry J Bean's ££ The large military and American expat presence has brought with it almost every fast food chain imaginable. This Tex-Mex eatery is one of the better ones. ⓐ Amari Resort, Thanon Beach ⓣ 03 842 8161 ⓛ 11.00–01.00

BARS & CLUBS

Hopf Brewery An in-house jazz band and on-site micro-brewery make this watering hole a cut above the rest. ⓐ 219 Thanon Beach ⓣ 03 871 0650 ⓛ 10.30–late

Shenanigans Considered to be the best expat bar in the city, Shenanigans offers genuine Irish beer and a friendly atmosphere. ⓐ The Avenue Pattaya, Pattaya 2nd Road ⓣ 03 872 3939 ⓦ www.shenanigansthailand.com ⓛ 10.00–late

THEATRE

Tiffany's A transvestite musical may not be top of your list of attractions, but you'll think again when you come to Pattaya. This resort city has some of the most glamorous and convincing *katoey* (transvestite) performers in Thailand. One of the biggest

Go to Pattaya if you like full-on nightlife

events of the year is the annual Miss Tiffany's contest, which is televised nationally. The crown is coveted by the cast of perfumed and made-up males. ⓐ 464 Thanon Pattaya 2 ⓣ 03 842 1700 ⓦ www.tiffany-show.co.th ⓛ Multiple performances every night. Admission charge

ACCOMMODATION

Rabbit Resort £–££ This beautiful property is located right on Jomtien Beach. Owned by a Thai-American couple, it is lovingly maintained and boasts immaculate rooms, each individually designed using Thai silks and artwork. Highly recommended. ⓐ Dongtan Beach, Jomtien ⓣ 03 830 3303 ⓦ www.rabbitresort.com

Cabbages & Condoms ££ It may be a strange name, but this delightful resort is actually part of a project that promotes sustainable development and health education. The views and gardens are a world away from the chaos of Pattaya. Condoms are given out free of charge in every room. ⓐ 366/11 Moo 12 Thanon Phra Tamnak 4, Nongprue, Banglamung, Chon Buri ⓣ 03 825 0556 ⓦ www.cabbagesandcondoms.co.th

Royal Cliff Beach Resort £££ The 5-star resort of Pattaya is packed with amenities, marble and gold fittings and fixtures. The residence of choice for those who like to make a statement every time they enter their suite. ⓐ 353 Thanon Phra Tamnak ⓣ 03 825 0421 ⓦ www.royalcliff.com

ⓞ *Bangkok's new Suvarnabhumi airport*

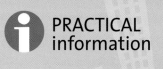

Directory

GETTING THERE
By air

The main gateway for international flights is Suvarnabhumi International Airport (see page 50). The airport opened in late 2006 and is now fully operational, although Don Muang Airport is still used for some domestic flights. Be sure to check arrival and departure airports carefully when planning flights in and out of as well as around the country. Airlines with regular schedules to Thailand include:

British Airways ☎ 0870 850 9850 ⓦ www.ba.com

Emirates ☎ 0870 243 2222 ⓦ www.emirates.com

EVA Air ☎ 020 7380 8300 ⓦ www.evaair.com

Qantas ☎ 0845 7747 767 ⓦ www.qantas.co.uk

Thai Airways International ☎ 0870 606 0911 ⓦ www.thaiair.com

Many people are aware that air travel emits CO_2, which contributes to climate change. You may be interested in the possibility of lessening the environmental impact of your flight through the charity **Climate Care** (ⓦ www.climatecare.org), which offsets your CO_2 by funding environmental projects around the world.

By rail

Travelling by rail is an excellent way to see the country – especially if you have plans to see the hill tribe regions of the north around Chiang Mai or if you want to combine your stay with visits to the southern resort regions. The only rail services that enter Thailand from a foreign country are those from

Singapore and peninsular Malaysia. Most major services terminate at Hua Lamphong Station.

State Railway of Thailand ☏ 02 222 0175 ⓦ www.railway.co.th

By road

Long-distance buses connect Bangkok with most of Southeast Asia – Burma being the major exception. This is the only way to enter or arrive from Cambodia or Laos if you don't fly.

Coaches also travel to and from the Golden Triangle region in the north and down to peninsular Malaysia and Singapore. Service levels vary incredibly depending on how much you pay. For long journeys go for VIP or even Super VIP which offer plenty of comfort.

There are three bus terminals that serve the country depending on the direction you are travelling to or from. Each is named according to the direction it serves.

Eastern Bus Terminal 🄰 300 Thanon Sukhumvit ☏ 02 391 8097 Ⓝ BTS: Ekkamai

Northern & Northeastern Bus Terminal 🄰 999 Thanon Kamphaengphet 2 ☏ 02 936 2852 Ⓝ MRT: Bang Sue

Southern Bus Terminal 🄰 147 Thanon Boromratchachonnani ☏ 02 435 5605 Ⓝ Not easily accessible by public transport

ENTRY FORMALITIES

Visitors to Thailand who are citizens of the UK, Ireland, the US, Canada, Australia and New Zealand are given permission to enter the country visa-free for up to 30 days upon arrival in the country. Passports valid for at least six months following arrival are required by all travellers, in addition to proof of an onward ticket out of the country. For up to date visa information, visit

the **Thai Ministry of Foreign Affairs** website (Ⓦ www.mfa.go.th).
Most personal effects and the following items are duty free:
200 cigarettes or 250 g of cigars or smoking tobacco, one litre
of wine or spirits, and photographic equipment (consisting of
one still, video or movie camera plus five rolls of still film or
three rolls of 8 mm or 16 mm motion-picture film).

Be warned that Thailand has strict controls regarding
narcotics, firearms and pornography. Don't even think of
transporting any such items into or out of the country.

MONEY

The currency in Thailand is the baht (B). A baht is divided into
100 satang. Currency denominations are: B1,000, B500, B100, B50
and B20 notes and coins of B10, B5, B1, 50 satang and 25 satang. Try to
get rid of large notes, or change them at your hotel, as they are not
taken by many merchants and taxi drivers due to a lack of change.

You can withdraw money using ATMs at almost all Thai banks.
Credit cards are widely accepted for almost all transactions, with
Visa, MasterCard and American Express the most common forms
of plastic. Always keep an eye on who is handling your cards in
order to avoid cloning scams. If you are given carbon copies of
slips, be sure to tear them up as soon as you receive them.

HEALTH, SAFETY & CRIME

It is advised, but not necessary, to get vaccinations for hepatitis
A and B, polio, rabies, typhoid and tuberculosis before arriving in
Thailand. Malaria is a possibility, but almost unheard of if you
stick to the city. Travel around the Burmese, Cambodian and
Laotian borders heightens your exposure to potentially malarial

regions and you should therefore take appropriate medication and precautions. During the wet season, dengue fever becomes an issue, so try to avoid being bitten by mosquitoes by using a good-quality repellent at all times. Also, keep covered up, especially in the evening, wear bright clothing and stay away from sources of stagnant water. Please note that there is no known cure for dengue fever, so once you see signs of a rash you should go to a doctor immediately.

Tap water is not advised unless you are in a 5-star resort or international-quality hotel. Ask in advance if your place of residence has a filtration system. Ice cubes are usually fine to have in drinks, even when served from street stalls, as ice is made with clean water in large factories. When in doubt, purchase a bottle of drink from the numerous street vendors. Try to avoid adding to the massive litter problem by recycling whenever possible.

Street food is one of the highlights of any visit to Thailand, but you should check dishes for quality before eating. If you see any sign of pinkness in poultry, do not eat it. If you are concerned in any way, stick to vegetarian dishes to stay safe.

Crimes against tourists are rare, but do occur. Pickpocketing and gem scams are the two most frequent incidents. Male 'guides' may also hassle you around major sights. If you have any problems, locate your nearest police office and the issue will disappear.

For details of emergency numbers, see page 138.

OPENING HOURS
Most government and private sector offices open 08.30–16.30 Monday to Friday. Shopping centres always stay open longer (from about 10.00–22.00).

Cultural institutions are usually open 08.30–16.00 Wednesday to Sunday, though opening hours are sometimes extended when major exhibitions hit town.

Banks have limited hours from 09.30–15.30 Monday to Friday. All nightclubs and bars close at 02.00, although underground venues do exist. Make friends with locals to find out where they are.

TOILETS
Public toilets are few in Bangkok – and those that do exist are positively foul. When you are caught short, head to the nearest shopping centre, department store or temple. You may have to spend a couple of baht for access. Always come prepared with toilet paper as it may not be provided. Many public conveniences will be squat-style with a plastic dipper used for cleansing.

CHILDREN
Bangkok is an extremely child-friendly city. The Thais love little kids and will smile at their cherubic faces at every opportunity. Safety, however, is another matter altogether. Pavements littered with potholes, chaotic drivers, choking traffic and a lack of access for those with buggies make it a difficult place to get around. Be sure to hold their hand all the time, as you never know when a speeding *tuk-tuk* will come around the corner.

Nappies and other baby supplies are readily obtained from supermarkets and drug stores.

There are a few things which will keep you – and the little ones – occupied whilst in town.

Children's Discovery Museum An activity and learning centre packed with games and exhibits galore. Everything is hands-on, including the live animal exhibits. ⓐ Thanon Kamphaengphet 4 ⓣ 02 615 7333 ⓦ www.bkkchildrenmuseum.com ⓛ 09.00–17.00 Tues–Fri, 10.00–18.00 Sat & Sun ⓝ BTS: Mo Chit; MRT: Chatuchak Park. Admission charge

Suan Siam (Siam Park) A great place to visit in summer. Waterslides, swimming pools and lazy rivers will cool both your body and your temper down. The park is located about 30 minutes east of the city in Bangkapi. ⓐ 101 Thanon Sukhapibarn 2, Bangkapi ⓣ 02 517 0075 ⓛ 10.00–18.00 Mon–Fri, 09.00–19.00 Sat & Sun ⓝ Bus: 26, 27. Admission charge

Technopolis Science Museum Even children who hate science will adore this interactive museum which features (hurrah!) English-speaking guides. ⓐ Techno Thani, Thanon Rangsit-Nakhon Nayok, Klong 5, Klong Luang, Pathum Thani ⓣ 02 577 9999 ⓦ www.nsm.or.th ⓛ 09.30–17.00 Tues–Sun ⓝ Bus: 44, 538 from Victory Monument; bus: 1155 from Rangsit. Admission charge

COMMUNICATIONS
Internet
Internet access is available almost everywhere, with cafés offering terminals all over the city. The Khao San Road, due to its huge backpacker population, is a good place to head for cheap, reliable and fast service.

Phones
Public phones accept coins or phonecards. Some pay phones

TELEPHONING THAILAND

The international calling code for Thailand is +66 and the area code for Bangkok is (0)2. To phone Bangkok from abroad, dial the international access code (usually 00) followed by 66, followed by 2, followed by the local number you require.

TELEPHONING ABROAD

To phone abroad from Thailand, dial Thailand's international access code (001), followed by the international calling code for the country you require, followed by the area code (leaving off the first '0'), followed by the local number. Some calling codes are: UK +44; Republic of Ireland +353; South Africa +27; Australia +61; New Zealand +64; Canada and the United States +1.

also accept credit cards for international calls. Local calls cost about B1 for every three minutes. Area codes must always be used in Thailand, even if you are calling from the same city.

Post

Postal services are quick and efficient. Stamps can be bought at any of the various post offices around the city, or from most convenience stores.

ELECTRICITY

The standard electrical current is 220 volts. Two-pin adaptors can be purchased at most electrical shops. Beware of shocks as plugs are unearthed.

TRAVELLERS WITH DISABILITIES

Facilities for visitors with disabilities are generally quite poor in Thailand. Pavements are riddled with cracks and there aren't any bevelled kerbs to assist with access. You will have to take your life into your hands by risking the street if you want to get around.

Some BTS stations have lifts. When in need, go to the nearest metro station to use the loo, as they will have accessible toilets.

For advice on travelling in Asia with a disability, contact **Disabled People's International** (ⓒ 02 503 4268 ⓦ www.dpiap.org).

TOURIST INFORMATION

The main branch of the Bangkok tourist office is located in Phra Nakon. There are also branches at three BTS stations: Nana, Saphan Taksin and Siam. They are an excellent source for maps, tours, directions to sights outside the city and other information.

Bangkok Tourist Bureau ⓐ 17/1 Thanon Phra Arthit ⓒ 02 225 7612 ⓦ www.bangkoktourist.com ⓛ 09.00–19.00 ⓝ Riverboat stop: Phra Arthit

BACKGROUND READING

Bangkok 8 by John Burdett. Fantastic crime thriller that combines Thai views on drug-use, religion, prostitution and race in one intoxicatingly pacy novel.

A History of Thailand by Chris Baker and Pasuk Phongpaichit. The full history of the country in one tome.

Sightseeing by Rattawut Lapcharoensap. This collection of short stories by Thailand's most celebrated modern writer gets under the skin of contemporary society.

Emergencies

EMERGENCY NUMBERS

For ambulance, fire brigade or police contact the Tourist Police on ☎ 1155 or the Tourist Assistance Centre on ☎ 02 281 5051.

MEDICAL EMERGENCIES

Many foreign nationals arrive in Thailand every year to take advantage of the cheap, yet high-quality health services provided in the country. Be sure to do your research as there are many fly-by-night operators. For serious emergencies, go directly to the emergency departments of the main public hospitals listed below, where there should be English-speaking doctors.

Bangkok Hospital Ⓐ 2 Soi Soonvijai 7, Thanon New Phetburi ☎ 02 310 3456 Ⓦ www.bangkokhospital.com Ⓝ MRT: Phra Ram 9

Bumrungrad Hospital Ⓐ 33 Soi Sukhumvit 3 ☎ 02 667 2999 Ⓦ www.bumrungrad.com Ⓝ BTS: Nana

Emergency pharmacies

Pharmacies are located throughout the city and many are open 24 hours. Many drugs normally available by prescription only back home can be picked up off the shelves at Thai pharmacies.

EMBASSIES & CONSULATES

American Embassy Ⓐ 120–122 Thanon Witthayu ☎ 02 205 4000 Ⓦ http://bangkok.usembassy.gov Ⓛ 07.00–16.00 Mon–Fri Ⓝ BTS: Phloen Chit

LOST PROPERTY

If you lose anything or suspect that it has been stolen, contact the police (see opposite). You will need to make a statement and fill in the required forms for insurance purposes.

Australian Embassy @ 37 Thanon Sathorn Tai ☎ 02 344 6300 🌐 www.austembassy.or.th 🕐 08.00–17.00 Mon–Fri ⓜ MRT: Lumphini

British Embassy @ 1031 Thanon Witthayu ☎ 02 305 8333 🌐 http://ukinthailand.fco.gov.uk 🕐 08.00–16.30 Mon–Thur, 08.00–13.00 Fri ⓜ BTS: Phloen Chit

Canadian Embassy @ 15th Floor, Abdul Rahim Place, 990 Thanon Rama IV ☎ 02 636 0540 🌐 http://geo.international.gc.ca/asia/bangkok 🕐 07.30–16.00 Mon–Thur, 07.30–13.00 Fri ⓜ BTS: Sala Daeng; MRT: Si Lom

Irish Embassy @ Ireland House, The Amp Walk, 218 Jalan Ampang, Kuala Lumpur, Malaysia ☎ +603 2161 2963 🌐 www.ireland-embassy.com.my 🕐 08.30–12.30 Mon–Fri

New Zealand Embassy @ 14th Floor, M-Thailand Building, 87 Thanon Witthayu ☎ 02 254 2530 🌐 www.nzembassy.com/Thailand 🕐 07.30–16.00 Mon–Fri ⓜ BTS: Phloen Chit

INDEX

SPOTTED YOUR NEXT CITY BREAK?

... then these CitySpots will have you in the know in no time, wherever you're heading.

Covering 100 cities worldwide, these vibrant pocket guides are packed with practical listings and imaginative suggestions, making sure you get the most out of your break, whatever your taste or budget.

Available from all good bookshops, your local Thomas Cook travel store or browse and buy online at www.thomascookpublishing.com

Thomas Cook Publishing

Editorial/project management: Lisa Plumridge
Copy editor: Monica Guy
Layout/DTP: Alison Rayner

The publishers would like to thank the following individuals and organisations for providing their copyright photographs for this book: Jacqueline Fryd, pages 21, 24, 27, 34, 42–3, 49, 51, 59, 67, 71, 73, 77, 83, 91, 96, 99 & 112; Pictures Colour Library, pages 15, 44–5, 105, 116, 125 & 127; World Pictures, pages 1, 7, 9, 11, 19, 23, 30–1, 39, 47, 87, 105, 120–1 & 129.

Send your thoughts to
books@thomascook.com

- Found a great bar, club, shop or must-see sight that we don't feature?
- Like to tip us off about any information that needs a little updating?
- Want to tell us what you love about this handy little guidebook and more importantly how we can make it even handier?

Then here's your chance to tell all! Send us ideas, discoveries and recommendations today and then look out for your valuable input in the next edition of this title.

Email the above address (stating the title) or write to: CitySpots Series Editor, Thomas Cook Publishing, PO Box 227, Coningsby Road, Peterborough PE3 8SB, UK.